Battle Orders • 13

The British Army in the Far East 1941–45

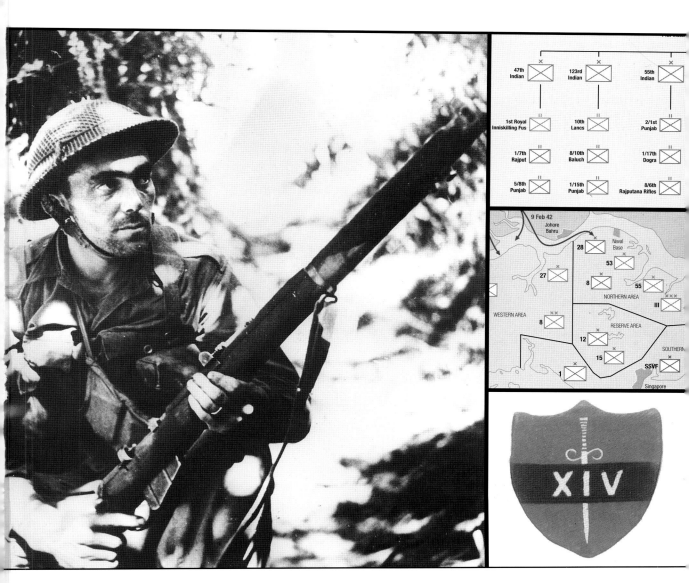

Alan Jeffreys • *Consultant editor Dr Duncan Anderson*

Series editors Marcus Cowper and Nikolai Bogdanovic

First published in Great Britain in 2005 by Osprey Publishing,
Elms Court, Chapel Way, Botley, Oxford OX2 9LP, United Kingdom.
443 Park Avenue South, New York, NY 10016, USA
Email: info@ospreypublishing.com

ISBN 1 84176 790 5

Editorial by Ilios Publishing, Oxford, UK (www.iliospublishing.com)
Design: Bounford.com
Maps by Bounford.com, Royston, UK
Index by Alison Worthington
Originated by PPS-Grasmere Ltd, Leeds, UK
Printed and bound in China through L-Rex Printing Company Ltd

05 06 07 08 09   10 9 8 7 6 5 4 3 2 1

A CIP catalogue record for this book is available from the British Library.

For a catalogue of all books published by Osprey Military and Aviation
please contact:
Osprey Direct, 2427 Bond Street, University Park, IL 60466, USA
E-mail: info@ospreydirectusa.com
Osprey Direct UK, P.O. Box 140, Wellingborough, Northants, NN8 2FA, UK
E-mail: info@ospreydirect.co.uk
www.ospreypublishing.com

Acknowledgements and image credits

I would like to thank Mike Taylor, Dr Daniel Marston and my
editor, Nikolai Bogdanovic, for all their help. I am particularly
indebted to my MPhil supervisor, Dr Tim Moreman, for all his
advice and help over the last few years. Finally thank you to my
family, Lorraine and Michael.

The photographs marked IWM are courtesy of the Imperial War
Museum, and can be ordered from the IWM's Film and
Photograph Archive in London.

Author's note

In the tree diagrams and maps in this volume, the units and forces
are distinguished by the following colours:

British	Brown
Japanese	Red
Indian	Blue
Australian	Green
African	Orange
Indian State Forces, Malays, and Burmese	Grey

For a key to the symbols used in this volume, see below.

Front cover main image A British Army corporal advances
cautiously at Ngakyedyauk Pass, with his SMLE rifle at the 'port'.
(Martin Brayley)

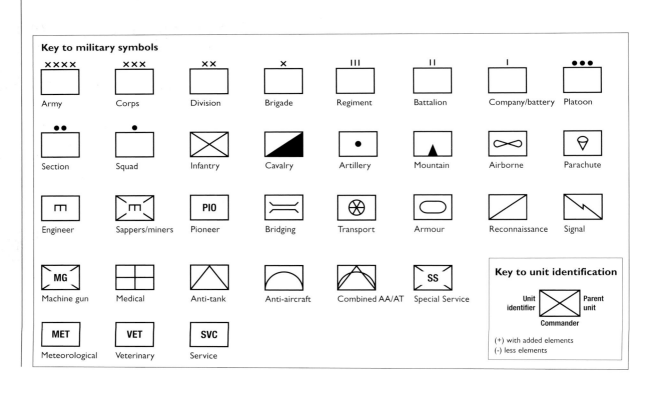

Key to military symbols

Contents

Introduction

From December 1941 to May 1942 the British Empire suffered the most humiliating series of defeats in its history, as Hong Kong, Malaya, Borneo, Singapore and Burma fell in rapid succession to the Imperial Japanese Army. The Fall of Singapore in February 1942 was considered by Winston Churchill 'the worst and largest capitulation in history'. The Japanese had overrun the numerically superior Commonwealth forces in Malaya in just over two months, resulting in 130,000 troops entering captivity. However, three years later the Japanese Army suffered defeat at the hands of the British and Commonwealth 14th Army at the Battles of Kohima and Imphal and in the battles for Burma. This transformation in the fortunes of the Commonwealth troops, in particular the Indian Army, was in a large part due to the development of jungle warfare doctrine and the resulting improvements in training, tactics and equipment.

These campaigns were largely fought in the jungle, an alien environment for most Commonwealth troops. The word 'jungle' is Indian in origin and means 'wasteland' but it has been used to describe anything from sparsely wooded areas to tropical forest. Until World War II the jungle was usually described as bush or forest in military circles. Generally there were two types of jungle: primary jungle, usually defined as natural jungle growth with poor visibility and little undergrowth, and secondary jungle, which was cleared jungle that had re-grown and consisted of very dense undergrowth, severely limiting movement. The jungle was filled with the problems of difficult climate, terrain, vegetation, wildlife and tropical disease such as malaria. Added to these were the tactical limitations imposed by the jungle, with its limited observation and fields of fire, communication problems, lack of mobility and long lines of supply. David Wilson, writing to his mother, commented on the jungle in Malaya:

> You can have no idea how thick the jungle is here, after one has left the road for ten or twenty paces, you cannot see the road at all and you have to rely entirely on your map to get you to the place that you are making for; a map is almost useless. The whole place is steaming wet, and one is soaked to the skin with the effort of pushing through the bush. A beastly place to have to fight in, if you didn't know it well.[1]

Troops could easily become bewildered, depressed and frightened in the jungle due to the strangeness of the terrain, emphasised by the limited visibility, the strange noises, the difficulty of movement and the sense of isolation in the jungle. This, in combination with the exhausting climate, made the conditions in Malaya and Burma extremely trying for the troops. These difficulties had to be overcome, before coming into contact with the enemy, through training and experience.

This book examines the training, tactics, organisation and equipment of the British Army in the Far East from 1941 until 1945. It mainly covers the conventional forces in theatre rather than the special forces such as the Chindits, V Force and Force 136. The development of the Commonwealth Armies in the Far East will be examined through the training manuals and pamphlets produced by GHQ India. This book also examines the dissemination of doctrine, the infantry divisions engaged in this theatre, and the tactics and equipment that they used, as well as the lessons learnt from the campaigns.

---

1 Letter to his mother, 14 September 1940, *Wilson Mss.*, Papers of Brigadier A. D. R. G. Wilson, IWM.

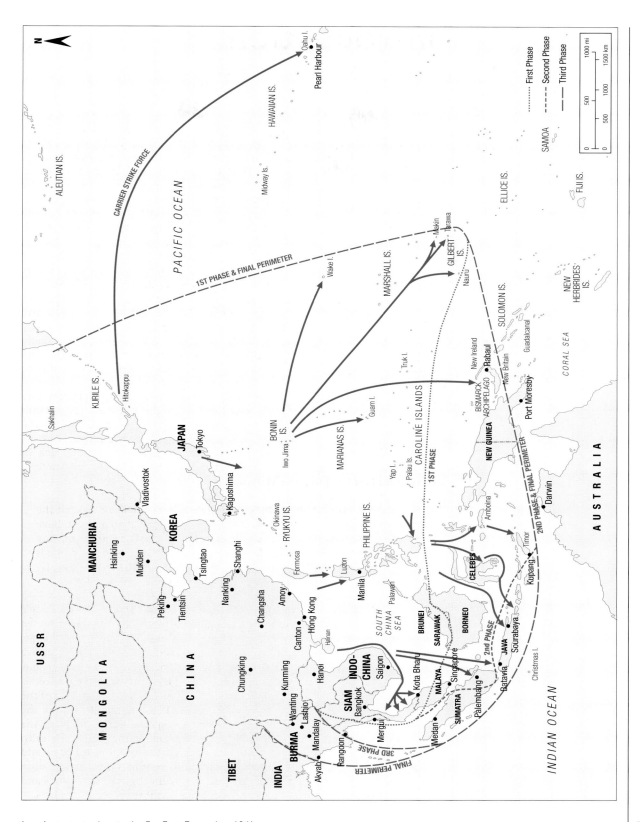

Japan's strategic plans in the Far East, December 1941.

5

Combat mission

During the 1920s and 1930s British strategy in the Far East centred upon the naval base at Singapore. Originally, the defence of Malaya and Singapore had been the responsibility of the Royal Navy. It was intended that in the event of an attack, the Navy would send a force from Britain and relieve the garrison of Singapore in 42 days; it was felt that any invading Japanese force could not overrun Malaya in this space of time. As far back as 1918, before the decision to build the naval fortress at Singapore had been taken, the question of landward defence of the Malayan mainland had been brought up by the then GOC of the Straits Settlement, Major-General Sir Dudley Ridout, in response to the growing Japanese purchase of land in the Malayan peninsula. The War Office took note of Ridout's report and recognised that further joint military and naval reconnaissance of the east coast of Malaya, and Johore in particular, was needed. The final paper proposing the development of the base at Singapore in 1921 stressed defence against a landward invasion as well as seaward attack. By 1924, however, The War Office took the view that the terrain was too difficult to traverse and as a result thought that there was no need for landward defences.

Lord Louis Mountbatten, Supreme Allied Commander, reads the order of the day from the steps of the municipal building in Singapore in 1945 after the surrender has been signed by the Japanese. (IWM)

This remained the official view until 1938 when the naval base was finally completed. The only role envisaged for the garrison was local defence and it trained accordingly using standard training manuals tailored for coastal defence.

This dominant view about the impracticality of an overland invasion through the jungles, swamps and plantations was challenged following the appointment of General Dobbie as GOC Malaya Command in 1935. In reference to the defence of Singapore, a report written in 1936 by Lieutenant-Colonel S. Woodburn Kirby, the future British official historian of the campaign, noted that the Malayan peninsula was neglected in military considerations. He was also critical of infantry training in Singapore, believing it suffered due to the climate and terrain. Colonel Arthur Percival, GSO1 Malaya in 1936, commented in a further report that training was along similar lines to the UK, where individual training was conducted from October to March and unit training was given from April to September. No mention was made of jungle training and nothing about the importance of acclimatisation.

The growing concern about landward defences was shared by other officers during the 1930s. Brigadier Vinden, who took up the post of GSO2 Malaya in 1937, challenged the idea that an invasion in the north of Malaya during the Monsoon season was impossible. He sailed up the coast and found Chinese junks

LEFT In 1941 III Indian Corps formed part of Malaya Command, and had its headquarters in Kuala Lumpur. In addition to its key 9th and 11th Indian divisions and the Lines of Communication troops, its organisation comprised Corps Troops, Federated Malay States Volunteer Forces, and Royal Army Medical Corps subunits. The other components of Malaya Command besides III Corps were Singapore Fortress troops, the British 18th Division, and the Australian 8th Division.

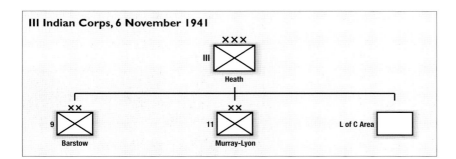

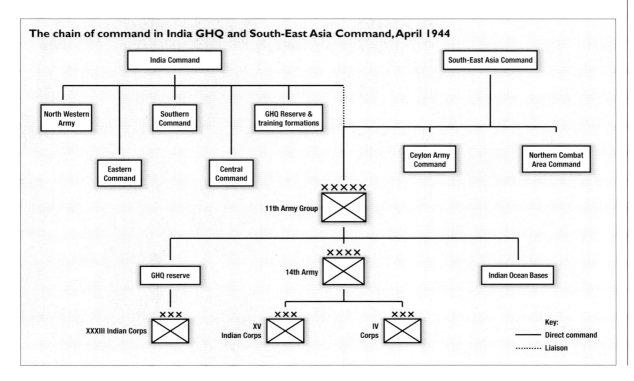

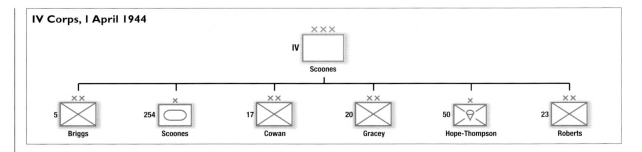

IV Corps, I April 1944

IV — Scoones

5 Briggs | 254 Scoones | 17 Cowan | 20 Gracey | 50 Hope-Thompson | 23 Roberts

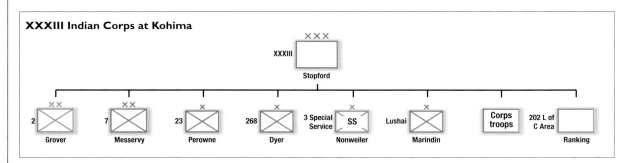

XXXIII Indian Corps at Kohima

XXXIII — Stopford

2 Grover | 7 Messervy | 23 Perowne | 268 Dyer | 3 Special Service SS Nonweiler | Lushai Marindin | Corps troops | 202 L of C Area Ranking

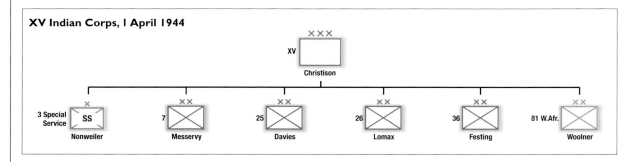

XV Indian Corps, I April 1944

XV — Christison

3 Special Service SS Nonweiler | 7 Messervy | 25 Davies | 26 Lomax | 36 Festing | 81 W.Afr. Woolner

landing on the east coast to avoid Malaya's immigration quotas. He also destroyed the myth of the impenetrable jungle by conducting an exercise with three British battalions and the Johore Defence Force against an attacking battalion of Gordon Highlanders. The Gordon's commanding officer had had jungle experience in West Africa. Vinden described how 'he sent his attack through the jungle considered impenetrable, and caught the defence in the rear. Another Malayan myth was destroyed.' To counteract this threat Vinden suggested an increase in the number of troops who 'would have to be trained in jungle warfare' about which even he knew little, he admitted. (Brigadier F.H. Vinden, *By Chance a Soldier*, unpublished memoir, IWM 96/36/1, pp.69–72, 77.)

The War in the Far East, which usually refers to the British and Commonwealth part of the larger Pacific War, began with the Japanese attack on Pearl Harbor on 7 December 1941, together with the attacks on Malaya, Hong Kong and the Philippines. The Japanese pre-emptive strikes enabled the capture of the natural resources they required from the European colonies of South-East Asia. In addition, the Japanese professed they wanted to create a Greater East Asia Co-Prosperity Sphere.

The outbreak of war meant that the defence of Singapore assumed far greater importance, since it formed the main bastion of the British Empire in the Far East against the Japanese threat. However, the time of relief had been extended from 40 to 180 days by 1941 and it had become clear that it was increasingly unlikely that the Royal Navy would be able to send out a fleet to Singapore while the threat from both the Italian and German navies remained in the European theatre. The burden of defence was initially placed on the Royal Air Force, with the Army defending the naval and air bases. However, in 1941 the RAF in the Far East had only 181 serviceable aircraft and 84 unserviceable ones, the majority of which were obsolescent. A figure of 566 frontline aircraft had been proposed as the minimum required for the defence of Malaya, and so it looked increasingly likely that the responsibility for the defence of Singapore, as well as that of mainland Malaya, would be placed in the hands of the Army. The few equipment supplies that were not needed by UK Home Forces were being sent to Russia; the Far East had the lowest priority after Europe, the Middle East and North Africa. Lastly with the fall of France in 1940, the Japanese would now be able to use Indo-China (modern-day Laos and Vietnam) to invade Burma, which was even more unprepared for war than Malaya and Singapore.

The United States took the leading role in the Pacific War, but it was made secondary to the war in Europe. This was confirmed at the first Washington Conference, which resulted in the shortlived ABDA (Amercian British Dutch Australian) Command under General Wavell. It was dissolved in March 1942, and in April, South-West Pacific Theatre Command was formed under General MacArthur. It was responsible for the Pacific Area, with Britain responsible for Burma, India, Malaya and Singapore.

In 1942, US strategy favoured the invasion of Northern Burma in order to re-open the Burma Road to aid Chaing Kai-Shek and their Chinese allies. The British Chiefs of Staff favoured the retaking of the Dutch East Indies, Malaya and Singapore as they knew from previous experience that a campaign in Burma would be drawn out due to the terrain and the climate. The newly-formed SEAC (South East Asia Command) in 1943 had the clear objectives of sweeping the Japanese forces from Burma, Malaya and South-East Asia and re-opening the Burma Road. However, the Americans mistrusted the motives of the British, nicknaming the Command 'Save England's Asiatic Colonies'. But by this stage the US no longer considered the China theatre of primary importance. US strategists wanted China to remain in the war and not to disintegrate into civil chaos, but it was felt that China contributed little to the final defeat of Japan and resources would be better used elsewhere. It is worth noting, though, that over half the Japanese Army was occupied in China throughout the war.

Doctrine and training

Preparing for jungle warfare

Prior to World War II, experience of fighting in the jungle was lacking in both the British and Indian armies as a whole. The knowledge that did exist was largely limited to those officers who had been hunting, also known as *shikar* or jungling, an activity often seen as one of the advantages of service in the Indian Army. This did not, however, amount to a viable doctrine. The British Army did not really come into contact with jungle conditions, and within the Indian Army only a few officers encountered the jungle through imperial policing in areas such as the jungles of Burma.

The most significant pre-war publication on jungle warfare was Charles Callwell's *Small Wars: Their principles and Practices*, whose second edition published in 1899 devoted a chapter to bush warfare against an irregular army. A range of books was also published at the turn of the century for soldiers fighting irregular opponents in Africa and Asia. In addition, there were the lessons learnt from the East African bush campaign during World War I, but these were not absorbed into training manuals, except for those produced for the African units of the Royal West African Frontier Force and the King's African Rifles. The only source of tactical guidance during the interwar period was the official doctrine used by all Commonwealth Armies laid down in the 1935 edition of *Field Service Regulations*, which devoted two pages to the subject of

Soldiers of the 2nd Battalion, Argyll and Sutherland Highlanders on the three-day march back from Mersing. (IWM K1076)

jungle warfare, focusing on operations against 'uncivilised' opponents. Jungle warfare on the North-East Frontier of India, during the interwar period for example, only affected paramilitary forces, such as the Burma Military Police and the Assam Rifles, fighting irregular opponents. Despite being officered by both British and Indian Army officers, none of the tactical lessons learned were disseminated into the mainstream of the British or Indian armies.

The defence of Malaya against a possible overland invasion (a growing threat through the 1930s) was the first indication that specialist knowledge of living, moving and fighting in the jungle might be required by regular British and Indian army troops. In 1940, the growing garrison of Malaya was given some guidance in the form of two pamphlets on jungle warfare produced in 1940; one issued by Malaya Command called *Tactical Notes for Malaya*, and the other by GHQ India entitled Military Training Pamphlet (MTP) No. 9 (India): *Notes on Forest Warfare*. The former discussed the problems of fighting in this environment and noted the importance of training in the jungle. It commented on the danger of malaria, the exhausting nature of the climate, and gave a good introduction to conditions in Malaya. It was issued to all Commonwealth troops arriving in Malaya and ominously noted the characteristics of the most likely enemy, the Japanese, highlighting their high standards of training, their amphibious landing skills, and their ruthlessness and powers of endurance. MTP No. 9 was written under the auspices of Colonel Sir Francis Tuker, DMT, in 1940, and copies were dispatched to Malaya. It was partly based on Tuker's bush experience, which was limited to 'uncivilised' opponents in Assam during 1919. The training manual was only 11 pages long and therefore only gave general guidelines for the bush of Asia and Africa, and was intended as an addendum to MTP. No. 5, *Notes on Extensive Warfare*. 'Extensive warfare' was defined as the more mobile warfare of smaller forces, in particular the infantry, with long lines of communication and fewer supporting weapons, in contrast to the intensive modern European warfare. Both pamphlets concentrated on the importance of infantry, mobility and the use of particular equipment such as machetes, sub-machine guns and 3in. mortars in jungle combat. Tactics for attack, defence and the counter-attack were explained: outflanking, small patrols, specialised equipment, mobile reserves, security against enemy penetration and speed of counter-attack were all examined. However, it is difficult to gauge how widely read the pamphlet was.

The actual progress being made in both jungle training and training in general by Commonwealth troops between 1940 and 1941 in Malaya was delayed by the building of defences (the main priority according to Malaya Command). For example, the 5/11th Sikh Regiment of 9th Indian Division arrived in Kuantan in April 1940. It consisted of 450 recruits and six ECOs (Emergency Commissioned Officers) who had joined the battalion a few weeks previously. As soon as it was ensconced in Kuantan it began defence work, despite the fact the unit was in dire need of basic training. Prior to the Japanese invasion the battalion had only undergone some platoon and company training and three 48-hour battalion schemes; no higher formation training had been attempted. A further setback was the fact that the ECOs could not speak the language of their soldiers.

Major Ian Stewart and the Argyll and Sutherland Highlanders

This lack of interest in carrying out hard, extensive training was partly the result of the underestimation of the Imperial Japanese Army by Malaya Command and the Intelligence Services. Thus, the amount of jungle training that was actually carried out by Commonwealth units largely depended on their role and the initiative of the individual commanders rather than any action by Malaya Command. The most notable exception was the 2nd

Battalion, Argyll and Sutherland Highlanders. The battalion was posted from India in 1939 and, together with the 4/19th Hyderabad Regiment and 5/2nd Punjabi Regiment, it formed 12th Indian Infantry Brigade. Major Ian Stewart assumed command of the battalion in 1940 and took a keen interest in training to fight in the jungle. He was instrumental in developing innovative ideas during early exercises in Johore after seeing the essential problems presented by jungle terrain, such as poor visibility, limited movement and the difficulties of command and control. Stewart made sure that all troops were integrated into his doctrine of jungle fighting, and even the pioneer and anti-aircraft platoons became experts. The Argylls' methods and training attracted publicity. In particular the march back to Singapore from Mersing, a distance of 61 miles that was achieved in three days, was widely reported in *The Straits Times*. In contrast, battalions such as the 2nd Gordon Highlanders packed up work at noon. Stewart was dismissed as a crank by some in Malaya Command and was nicknamed 'Mad Stewart', an opinion reinforced by his abrasive character that alienated much support. As a result Malaya Command did not act upon his

India and South-East Asia showing where the key training establishments mentioned in the text were located. The training centres are indicated within boxes.

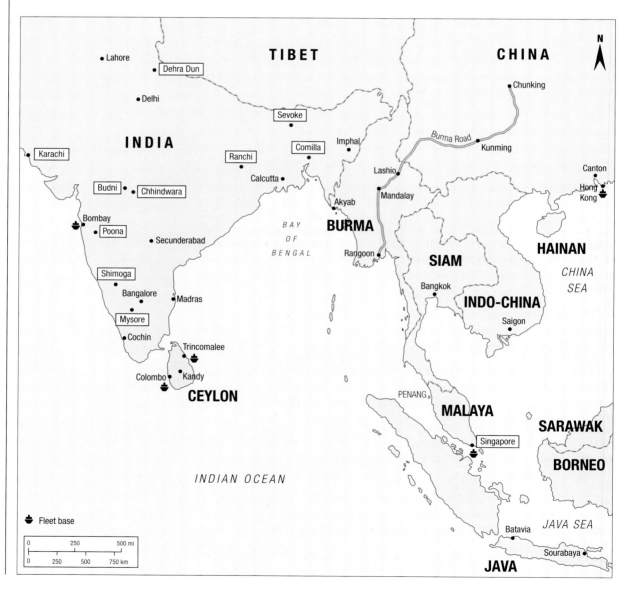

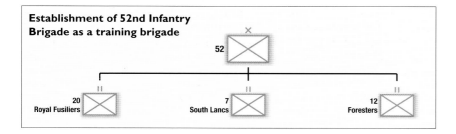

Establishment of 52nd Infantry
Brigade as a training brigade

52

20 Royal Fusiliers

7 South Lancs

12 Foresters

innovative ideas on jungle warfare. However, his methods were recognised in other quarters. Four Argylls joined 101st Special Training School as instructors, for 'behind the lines' work in the jungle, and two officers joined the Officer Cadet Training Unit as jungle warfare instructors.

The appointment of Lieutenant-General Arthur Percival as GOC Malaya Command in May 1941 led to an increase in the tempo of training in Malaya following completion of the defence works. Percival had served during the interwar period with the Royal West African Frontier Force, one of the few regiments with a tradition of bush warfare both for internal security and fighting a conventional army during World War I. This experience, in combination with his time in Malaya Command during 1936–37, made him the ideal candidate to promote jungle training. Thus, training was encouraged and training manuals were available – but there was not enough time to train properly before the Japanese invasion to put it all into practice.

In contrast to the Malayan Garrison, the Japanese army preparing to invade Malaya was a hardened fighting force with recent experience in China. Although amphibious training had been studied, the IJA had no experience of jungle warfare nor a doctrine for how to conduct it. At the beginning of 1941 Colonel Masanobu Tsuji was involved in researching jungle warfare in Taiwan. He ended the year as Director of the Planning and Operations Staff of the invading 25th Army. A pamphlet was produced called *Read This Alone – And The War Can Be Won* for Japanese troops destined for Malaya, which contained useful information on jungle conditions. The Japanese 5th Division did not begin to train for the invasion of Malaya until 15 August 1941. Therefore, the strength of the Japanese Army lay in its status as a battle-hardened and well-disciplined force, rather than in being specifically trained in jungle warfare.

The lessons from Burma and Malaya

In Burma, the problem of fighting in the jungle had been previously studied and practised by paramilitary units. There had been intermittent jungle operations against hill tribes in the border areas from the 19th century up until and during the early years of World War II. The paramilitary forces in Burma consisted of the Burma Military Police (BMP) and the Burma Frontier Force (BFF). The BMP had a long tradition of maintaining internal security and in this role had been involved in jungle warfare against irregular tribesman since 1886. Lessons were encapsulated in a training manual in 1902, which was revised in the 1920s, called the *Manual of Jungle Warfare for the Officers of the Burma Military Police*. There is little to suggest that the lessons learned were absorbed by the British Army, but the experience was disseminated by word of mouth among BMP officers, who were Indian Army officers on temporary loan to the Burma Army. The BFF was an offshoot of the BMP, whose purpose was the internal security of the mainly jungle tribal areas. Its troops were also trained in jungle warfare because they spent most of their time in the jungles of the North-East Frontier and were recruited from tribesmen brought up in this environment, as well as some Indian and Gurkha soldiers.

Lessons from the campaigns in Malaya and Burma were included in the third edition of MTP No. 9 in August 1942. It was considerably larger than the first edition, with an increase from 11 to 73 pages and now had a distribution of 45,000 copies to all the officers of the Indian and British Armies and NCOs of the British Army in India. It stressed that the Japanese were not 'supermen' and that British, Australian, Indian and Gurkha troops had all proved this. The new edition included a section on Japanese tactical methods, which were described at length but were summed up in four words: mobility, speed, infiltration and encirclement. Other sections focused on attack and defence for all arms against Japanese tactics, ambushes, patrols, administrative problems, minor tactics and training. For attack, encircling and filleting were the two suggested methods and aggressive patrols and ambushes were to be used in both attack and defence. The idea of the defensive boxes were adapted from the 'box doctrine' developed in North Africa:

> Our boxes will, therefore, be placed astride the enemy's lines of approach. They must be made as strong as possible artificially with wire, mines booby traps, automatic fire, etc. – in order to economize men. They must be fully stocked to withstand a siege. They must be in depth along the L. of C. so that if the enemy by-passes the first he will bump into the second and so on, and so that he can be squeezed between them by counter-attack from each side.[2]

Because the jungle was alien to nearly all the fighting troops, they needed practical training in order to master this new terrain. Training was divided up

British soldiers training for jungle warfare in full equipment.
(IWM IND 1555)

2 MTP (India) No. 9 *Jungle Warfare* 3rd edition, August 1942, p. 26.

into four areas of jungle craft: map reading and the use of the compass to find one's way in the jungle; concealment; jungle lore; and use of weapons to achieve maximum effect. However, the pamphlet perpetuated the myth that Japanese were short-sighted, and its concealment hints were taken from Baden-Powell's *Scouting for Boys*. Thus by the end of 1942, the Indian High Command had made some progress in disseminating jungle warfare doctrine and implementing appropriate training, especially with the publication of the third edition of MTP No. 9, but more notice and practical application of the training manual was necessary for the jungle warfare training to succeed. However, there was still a lack of co-ordination and individual divisions imposed their own training regimes, with little centralised control.

The Army in India was unable to concentrate entirely on preparing for jungle warfare, as the strategic situation meant that that GHQ India also provided troops during the early years of the war for campaigns in the Middle East and North Africa. There was also substantial unrest in India during this period and many battalions were assigned to internal security duties. The Cripps Mission and the resultant 'Quit India' movement in the summer of 1942 was the most serious and it took 57 infantry battalions to deal with the disturbances. Much of the trouble occurred in the Eastern Army's province and thus training for the war against the Japanese was delayed. Airfield construction, factory production of arms, clothing and equipment were similarly retarded. In addition, the monsoon of 1942 had been very heavy and was followed by a terrible malaria epidemic on the lines of communication to units in North-East India. For instance, it had decimated a whole transport company by the end of September and the casualty rate for malaria on the Imphal front was 600 per cent. There were also disturbances by the Hurs, a Muslim sect in Sind, and a *lashkar* (tribal war party) influenced by the Fakir of Ipi creating problems on the North-West Frontier. Thus large numbers of troops were directed to aid the civil powers and were unable to train.

The June 1943 Infantry Committee

The real turning point, as far as improving overall standards of jungle training was concerned, was the appointment of the Infantry Committee in June 1943 on the orders of the C-in-C India after the disastrous First Arakan campaign had shown how dire the situation was. It was a direct result of the disastrous First Arakan operation with a brief to look at the standards of the British and Indian infantry battalions in India and to make recommendations for their improvement. There was an impressive amount of operational and administrative experience among the members of the Committee, who included the DMT, Major-General R. D. Inskip, Major-General H. L. Davies (recently appointed GOC 25th Indian Division and who had been chief of staff to Generals Hutton and Slim) and Major-General J. M. L. Grover (GOC, 2nd Division). The Committee studied the problem for two weeks. It blamed the defeats in Burma and Malaya on the 'milking' and expansion of the Indian Army, the failure to recognise the importance of infantry in battle, the lack of basic training and experienced leadership, the fighting on two fronts, the lack of collective training as formations, prolonged periods of contact with the enemy, the lack of trained reinforcements, the problem of malaria, and the lack of resources.

The Infantry Committee's proposed solution was thorough basic training of recruits, which would be followed by a period of jungle training for both British and Indian troops. It had become apparent that Regimental Training Centres were unable to deal with all the basic training needs. The 13th Frontier Force Regiment, for example, had 14 active battalions organised, equipped and armed in six different ways. The Committee accepted the DMT's proposal that training divisions be set up in order to teach jungle warfare after basic training. All Indian troops and British reinforcements would now undergo two months

The front cover of Military Training Pamphlet No.52, *Warfare in the Far East (Provisional)*, December 1944. The topics covered within this training manual include topography, jungle-craft, general tactics, medicine and hygiene, intercommunication, and training for jungle warfare. The Appendices also provide information on the terrain, climate vegetation and wildlife of the major countries in the Far East where British and Commonwealth troops were expected to fight, together with a brief outline of Japanese tactics.

Military Training Pamphlet No. 52 3?

Warfare in the Far East
(Provisional)

1944
This pamphlet supersedes the 1942 Edition of MTP No. 52

RESTRICTED

The information given in this document is not to be communicated, either directly or indirectly, to the Press or to any person not authorized to receive it

Prepared under the direction of the Chief of the Imperial General Staff

THE WAR OFFICE   DECEMBER 1944

CROWN COPYRIGHT RESERVED

26/GS Publications/1335

jungle training under designated training divisions. Other recommendations included the end of 'milking', increasing the pay of both British and Indian infantry, improving the training of the infantry with other arms, steps to improve the quality of officers and NCOs and improving the reinforcement system. Collective training and co-operation with other arms as well as with the RAF were also recommended. Finally, the need for a definitive jungle warfare doctrine was highlighted.

The campaigns in Malaya, Burma and First Arakan had shown that MTP No. 5 on *Extensive Warfare* and the existing training manuals for jungle warfare were an inadequate basis for infantry training, as the manuals did not fully address new tactical problems such as bunkers. It was not until after the Arakan that periodic Army in India Training Memorandum (AITMs) regularly included sections on jungle warfare and specific training for warfare in this terrain. In conjunction with the different editions of MTP No. 9 this shows the steady development of thinking on jungle warfare from 1940 onwards. However, as AITM No. 20 stated in April 1943:

> Field craft, section formations and patrolling are the essentials for success in all forms of warfare but attain added importance in the jungle. Every officer and NCO professes to have read and mastered MTP 14 (India) [on Infantry Section Leading] and MTP 33 (Home) yet experience shows that they seldom if ever put into practice the most elementary principles contained in these publications.[3]

Thus it was apparent that many officers had not read the training manuals or carried out training according to their guidelines. However, in accordance with the directives from GHQ India the AITMs gave increasing coverage to jungle warfare from AITM No. 20 onwards, which noted the importance of health discipline, jungle lore and minor tactics in jungle warfare.

The Indian Army produced several new or revised training pamphlets dealing with jungle fighting during 1943. There had been a tradition of using battle drill in the Indian Army since pre-1914 for fighting on the North-West Frontier. *Battle Drill for Thick Jungle 1943,* which would complement MTP No. 9, laid down battle drill for sections, platoons and companies. It stated that 'every private soldier must now be something of a tactician' and it was considered that the drill would help develop the initiative of the soldiers. In contrast, battle drill in the UK was thought to stifle initiative.

The Jungle Book, 1943

GHQ India finally produced a comprehensive jungle warfare doctrine with the publication of 80,000 copies of the fourth edition of MTP No. 9 (India), *The Jungle Book*, in September 1943. The new edition had doubled the circulation of the previous editions of MTP No. 9. It had a new format that according to General Auchinleck was to be different from the usual, dull training manuals and was aimed at popularising training. It included photographs and cartoons for the first time in order to make it more appealing to officers and men. Its clearly stated purpose was to help COs train their units in the specialised fighting methods needed to beat the IJA in the jungle, stating: 'In principle there is nothing new in jungle warfare, but the environment of the jungle is new to many of our troops. Special training is therefore necessary to accustom them to jungle conditions and to teach them jungle methods'.[4] It gave the examples of jungle craft, physical fitness, good marksmanship and decentralised control as attributes that needed addressing in jungle warfare training.

The training manual assimilated all the lessons from the previous editions of MTP No. 9 and the AITMs, and included lessons from First Arakan and from American and Australian experiences of fighting the Japanese in

The cover of *The Jungle Book* training manual, the first popularised jungle-warfare training pamphlet produced by a professional production team employed by the Directorate of Military Training in India. The pamphlet was meant to be readable and appealing to wartime officers and men, hence the Japanese caricature on the cover and the liberal use of photographs throughout the text.

MILITARY TRAINING PAMPHLET No. 9 (INDIA)
4TH EDITION—SEPTEMBER 1943

3 AITM No. 20, April 1943, Appendix D, p. 21.
4 MTP No. 9, *The Jungle Book*, 4th edition, (Sept, 1943), p. 1.

the Pacific. The pamphlet was the basis of jungle fighting methods for the remainder of World War II. It was by no means perfect, however, and was intended to be developed and improved. AITM No. 24 commented on *The Jungle Book*'s excellent notes on attack, but the section needed to be amplified. Indeed, it later formed the basis for two War Office manuals in 1944–45 (Military Training Pamphlet No. 51, *Preparation for Warfare in the Far East*, June 1945, 2nd edition; and Military Training Pamphlet No. 52, *Warfare in the Far East*, December 1944) demonstrating that it was the Indian Army rather than the British Army that pioneered jungle warfare doctrine.

The Jungle Book was to be used in collaboration with another pamphlet, *Japanese in Battle – Enemy Methods*, which highlighted Japanese tactics. This pamphlet was a detailed observation of the IJA in Burma and the South-West Pacific. It noted the use of surprise, mobility and offensive action by the Japanese in these theatres. It also showed the Japanese tactics in attack, with examples, but the majority of the pamphlet was given over to their mutually supporting defensive systems, again listing examples and in particular bunkers in the First Arakan. *The Jungle Book* together with the other ancillary training manuals became the focus for the dissemination of doctrine in India and for all units and formations preparing for war in Burma.

The formation of training divisions

The main thrust for training in India now emphasised jungle warfare, overseen by the new C-in-C, General Sir Claude Auchinleck, who implemented the proposals of the Infantry Committee. The 14th and 39th Indian divisions were chosen as the training divisions and were withdrawn to reorganise. The 14th Division, which had served on the North-East Frontier during 1942 and in the

A British soldier sighting his 2in. mortar during training. The 2in. mortar could fire high-explosive, smoke or illuminating ammunition and had a range of 100–150 yds. It remained in service for 25 years after World War II. (IWM IND 1811)

First Arakan campaign, was now based at Chhindwara. The 39th Light Division, formerly the 1st Burma Division, had been involved in the retreat from Burma and had been training for jungle warfare for six months in areas of extensive jungle before being relocated to Saharanpur. British infantry reinforcements were trained in jungle warfare by the new 52nd Brigade at Budni in Bhopal State, after a spell of basic training with the 13th Battalion, The Sherwood Foresters, at Jubbulpore.

After two months in the training divisions the recruits were sent to the reinforcement camps, where training continued until they could join their battalions. The rest and reinforcement camps were reorganised under Colonel J. H. Gradige. They had been set up in April 1943 on the example of those in the Middle East and were designed to hold and train 3,000 troops. The instructors were from India, often with little experience of frontline conditions, and ratios of instructors to troops were very low with little direction for training, all resulting in poor morale and cases of ill discipline. After August 1943, each camp was allocated to a particular division, divisional flags were flown in the camps and formation signs were worn, helping the reinforcements feel they were already part of the division and improving morale. In addition, realistic training was undertaken and discipline was restored.

The Indian High Command ensured that jungle warfare training formed the main focus of all training carried out by units, formations and at training establishments throughout India. The syllabus for the Tactical School at Poona, where officers learnt the latest tactical doctrine, now included large sections dealing with jungle training. The work of specialised training establishments already dealing with jungle fighting was stepped up. The Jungle Warfare School at Comilla, initially run by 14th Indian Division, moved to Sevoke near Darjeeling in Northern Bihar in 1943 and was run by Major Parry of the 2/5th Gurkha Rifles and Major Firth. Each course lasted for 15 days and demonstrated new tactics required for jungle warfare to British and Indian officers and other ranks. The course not only covered jungle training but also a period of battle inoculation to accustom students to the noise and confusion of battle. As Captain Morris commented, having undertaken the instruction:

> This course is partly to train people to fight in the jungle, and partly to get people accustomed to being fired at. For the first few days we had a pretty strenuous time, doing attacks and bayonet fighting and obstacle courses etc., and always firing real ammunition. The enemy is usually dummies, but the instructors fired at us quite a bit and let off bombs and things to make everything more realistic.[5]

The syllabus included patrolling, living off the land, fire control, minor tactics, preparation of road blocks and other obstacles, house to house fighting, camouflage, use of small craft, explosives, booby traps and jungle lore. It finished with a three-day course in the jungle. Lessons learnt at the school were then taken back to the battalion by officers and ensured these ideas were put into practice. However, according to AITM No. 22 published in August 1943, which commented on the jungle warfare course at Sevoke, VCOs and NCOs were still having difficulty with fire control in the jungle and were very wary of the terrain that few of them had encountered before. Other criticisms included a lack of compass work and that students were surprised by the physical and mental strain that the jungle imposed on them. It was also perceived that the contents of the course were not being absorbed by the parent units, which failed to take advantage of men trained as instructors at GHQ Jungle Warfare Schools. Due to the demand for places on the course a second jungle warfare school was opened at Shimoga in November 1943.

---

5 Letter from Captain C. A. Morris, 14 August 1943, *Morris Mss.*, IWM 99/22/1

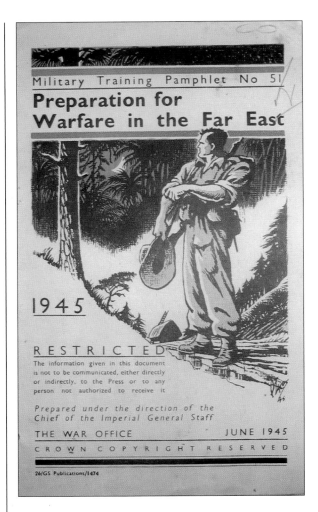

Military Training Pamphlet No. 51

Preparation for Warfare in the Far East

1945

RESTRICTED

The information given in this document is not to be communicated, either directly or indirectly, to the Press or to any person not authorized to receive it

Prepared under the direction of the Chief of the Imperial General Staff

THE WAR OFFICE   JUNE 1945

CROWN COPYRIGHT RESERVED

26/GS Publications/1474

Military Training Pamphlet No. 51, *Preparation for Warfare in the Far East* (June 1945). This training manual was produced by the War Office for British troops earmarked for the Far East after the war in Europe was over.

The existing Jungle Warfare Training Centre at Raiwala Bara, near Dehra Dun, was initially set up by Major Angus Rose in December 1942 to train Indian reinforcements destined for Eastern Army, but it had never functioned properly in its assigned role. Following the formation of the training divisions it was now given the role of training complete units or cadres in jungle warfare skills. For example, all three battalions of the newly formed 50th Indian Parachute Brigade were trained at Raiwala. The chief instructor was Major James of the Middlesex Regiment and V Force, who had served in the retreat from Burma. The training comprised three stages. The first week consisted of drills for jungle manoeuvres and different types of ambush. The second week comprised training schemes for all-day and all-night fighting. The final week consisted of two separate two-day exercises. Overall, training proved invaluable when the battalion was caught up in the fighting at Sangshak in March 1944.

The threat posed by malaria had clear training implications that were also addressed by India Command. For example, a medical school of jungle warfare was set up in July 1943 by 26th Indian Division in Arakan and was attended by officers from all the other divisions based in North-East India. Medical advances had ensured that malaria could be contained through insecticides, anti-malarial discipline and mepracrine, although casualties remained a problem. Medical officers were being trained in anti-malarial measures by October and anti-malarial works sections were set up to counter the problems in Assam by improving drainage. Anti-malarial discipline was strictly enforced and, by late-1943, these measures had proved to be largely successful. The drill was originally adopted by 23rd Indian Division and later adopted by all operational formations. Malaria rates were also high in jungle-warfare training areas. To combat this a policy was adopted whereby training should be restricted to non-malarial areas in Northern India where the malaria season was short. In the centres that could not be relocated, such as the Jungle Warfare Training School at Managade in Mysore, a comprehensive malaria control scheme was enforced. Malaria casualties in forward areas were now treated at the Malarial Forward Treatment Units, and thus the lines of communication were less affected by malaria casualties.

Training continued after the battles of Kohima and Imphal as units and formations prepared for the next phase of the fighting and lessons of the recent fighting were absorbed into later editions of the AITMs. The development of training and tactical methods was a continuous process and new reinforcements had to be absorbed into units. Training manuals for jungle warfare were now in abundance. Other feedback from the front included *Battle Bulletins*, which comprised first-hand accounts of patrolling, operations and fighting.

Divisional organisation

In the Commonwealth armies during World War II, apart from Higher Commands, the structure started with an army-level unit. In this particular theatre, from 1943 onwards it was the 14th Army. In an army there are usually two or three corps and three divisions within a corps. An army division was composed of three brigades of three battalions, one of which would be a British Army battalion in an Indian Army division.

All the divisions bar one that fought in this theatre were infantry divisions. There were three British divisions in theatre, namely the regular British Army 2nd Division, 18th Division and the 36th Division. There were also two West African divisions and the 11th East African Division, all led by British officers and NCOs. One Australian division fought in Malaya and two Canadian regiments in Hong Kong. The majority of the Commonwealth troops were provided by the Indian Army, which contributed 13 infantry divisions and one airborne division in South-East Asia. As Major-General Henry 'Taffy' Davies, Commander of 25th Indian Division, commented in his memoir:

14th Army's formation badge. It was designed by Slim himself, but was only adopted after an open competition. The red and black represented the colours of the British and Indian armies and the sword pointed downwards, against heraldic convention, because Slim knew that the 14th Army would have to re-conquer Burma from the north. The hilt formed the 'S' for Slim and on the handle was the army's title in morse code.

> The Division, as all soldiers know, is the basic fighting formation in practically every army in the world. It is large and powerful enough with its establishment of about 17,000 men, to effect a decisive influence in any military operation, irrespective of the scale of campaign. At the same time, it is sufficiently compact to enable its commander to exercise a personal leadership and control and to permit its functioning as a well co-ordinated team. In the British Army, during two world wars, the Divisional spirit has been something which has been fostered and nourished as an important matter of principle.[6]

However, in the Far East as elsewhere, the fundamental loyalty of the soldier was to his immediate peer group and typically to his own infantry section.

In 1941, the war establishment of British and Commonwealth Army infantry divisions usually consisted of three infantry brigades of three infantry battalions plus three artillery field regiments, one anti-tank regiment, one light anti-aircraft regiment, three engineer field companies, one field park company and divisional signals. This developed throughout the war according to the theatre the division was fighting in. The Indian Army prior to World War II had largely been organised for the roles of imperial policing on the North-West

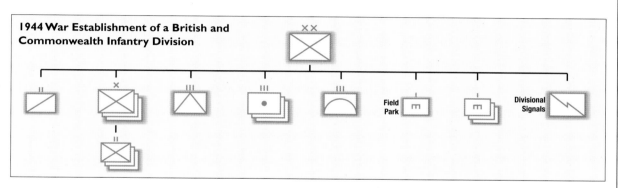

1944 War Establishment of a British and Commonwealth Infantry Division

Field Park

Divisional Signals

---

6 Major-General H. L, Davies, 'Small Green Men' (unpublished memoir), p. 126, IWM 66/82/1.

21

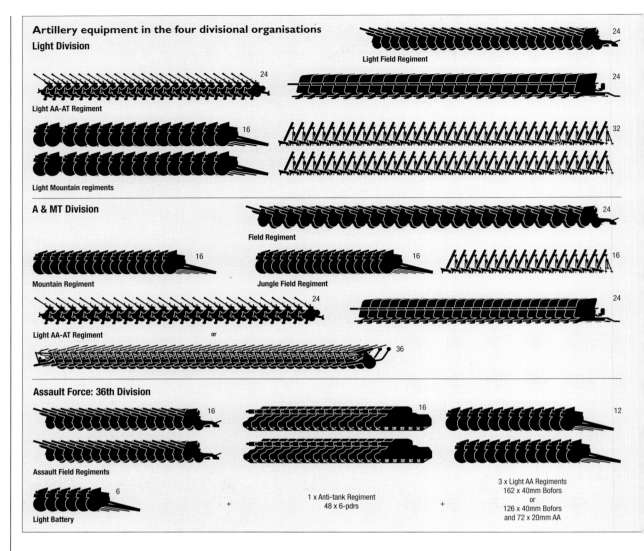

Artillery equipment in the four divisional organisations

Light Division

Light Field Regiment — 24

Light AA-AT Regiment — 24

— 24

Light Mountain regiments — 16

— 32

A & MT Division

Field Regiment — 24

Mountain Regiment — 16

Jungle Field Regiment — 16

— 16

Light AA-AT Regiment — 24   or

— 24

— 36

Assault Force: 36th Division

Assault Field Regiments — 16

— 16

— 12

Light Battery — 6

+

1 x Anti-tank Regiment
48 x 6-pdrs

+

3 x Light AA Regiments
162 x 40mm Bofors
or
126 x 40mm Bofors
and 72 x 20mm AA

Frontier and internal security. Therefore, even with its expansion and the resultant 'milking' of existing units, it was in need of reorganisation to fight the IJA. The highest formation in India in 1939 was a brigade.

Each standard infantry battalion normally had four rifle companies as well as support weapons. Each company, in turn, was split into three platoons and each platoon into three sections of about ten men or less, but usually more than six. Even within the section a soldier usually had a 'mucker' or mate with whom he 'brewed up', the pair looking after each other in and out of action. This was the usual foundation for comradeship among all soldiers and kept individuals going through the tremendous hardships of fighting the Japanese and the jungle. This is well depicted in George MacDonald Fraser's *Quartered Safe Out Here*, and highlighted by the 2nd and 36th Divisions' historian:

> In Burma, more than in any other theatre, it was an infantryman's war, and it was the section, the platoon and the company that won the many small victories which, added together, made the campaigns the successes they were.[7]

7 Anon., *The Amalgamation of 2 and 36 Divisions. War Histories 1939–1945*, IWM K. 83492.

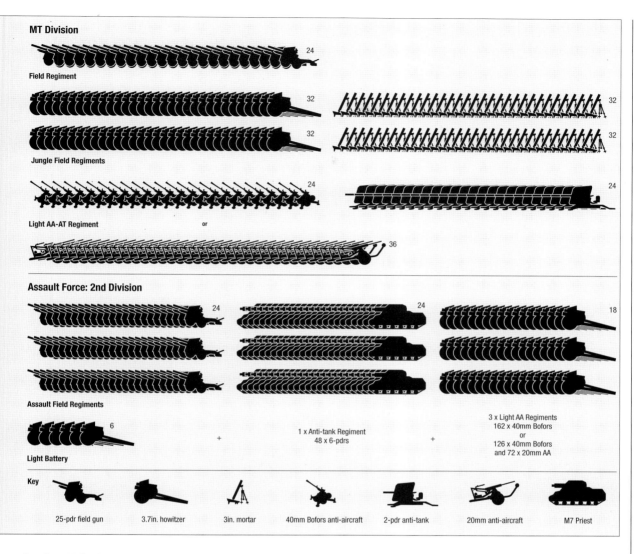

MT Division

Field Regiment — 24

Jungle Field Regiments — 32, 32, 32, 32

Light AA-AT Regiment — 24, 24 or 36

Assault Force: 2nd Division

Assault Field Regiments — 24, 24, 18

Light Battery — 6

+ 1 x Anti-tank Regiment 48 x 6-pdrs +

3 x Light AA Regiments
162 x 40mm Bofors
or
126 x 40mm Bofors
and 72 x 20mm AA

Key

25-pdr field gun | 3.7in. howitzer | 3in. mortar | 40mm Bofors anti-aircraft | 2-pdr anti-tank | 20mm anti-aircraft | M7 Priest

In the 14th Army as a whole, no matter whether the troops were African, British or Indian, there was a belief that the soldiers were fighting a worthy cause not merely to defend India and reoccupy Burma, but to defeat the Imperial Japanese Army as an 'evil force'. Loyalty to the 14th Army and the individual British, Indian and African divisions was fostered through the use of formation badges, training and going into action together.

After the 1942 retreat from Burma, reorganisation within the divisional structure was instigated in response to the over-reliance on roads in the recent campaigns. The number of vehicles was reduced in the 7th, 20th and 23rd Indian divisions, which were renamed Mixed Transport divisions and later called Animal and Mechanised Transport divisions (A & MT) rather than MT divisions. The 17th and 39th Indian divisions were converted to Light divisions of two brigades, with six mule companies and four jeep companies each, in order to be able to operate away from the road. Other changes in the Light Divisions included abolishing the anti-aircraft and gun platoons in the British units. The gun platoon was replaced by a medium machine-gun platoon.

The lessons of the First Arakan also brought about changes in organisation of divisions fighting in the jungle. These included the formation of one artillery regiment in each division specifically as a jungle field regiment. Two batteries were equipped with eight jeep-towed 3.7in. howitzers (modified with pneumatic-tyre wheels for towing) and the third battery with sixteen 3in. mortars to give artillery support where 25-pdr field artillery guns could not be used. Thus, the jungle field regiment could operate away from the roads, and mountain regiments would operate where jeeps could not be used. Light Anti-Aircraft and Anti-Tanks regiments were also combined for fighting in the jungle to make one Anti-Aircraft and Anti-Tank Regiment with two batteries each of twelve 6-pdrs and the other two batteries each of eighteen 20mm anti-aircraft guns. In the MT and A & MT divisions, British and Indian battalions were reorganised to consist of battalion HQ, HQ company containing signals, mortar, carrier and pioneer platoons, an administrative company containing medical and transport platoons and four rifle companies.

In 1944 there were four distinct divisional organisations in India: the MT Division, the A & MT Division, the Light Division and the Assault Division. This was standardised in a conference at GHQ India on 26–27 May 1944, during the Battle of Imphal, and was also influenced by the recommendations of the Lethbridge Mission of June 1943 (see the *Weapons and equipment* chapter). All divisions were now required to have a divisional HQ defence battalion. The Lethbridge report recommended that this did not have to be a permanent arrangement and the battalion could be exchanged at intervals with a battalion from one of the infantry brigades. It also recommended that each division have a reconnaissance battalion of Light Infantry that would be of similar organisation to an infantry battalion bar the medium machine gun and 3in. mortar platoons, with an increase in the signals platoon and the dropping of one company. The battalion would, therefore, have a battalion HQ, a HQ company consisting of company HQ, signal platoon, transport platoon, administrative platoon and a pioneer platoon, with three rifle companies with company HQ and four platoons. This would enable the reconnaissance battalion to be extremely mobile and to work independently of the parent unit for long periods at a time.

In addition, each division was allocated a medium machine-gun battalion, as a result of the experiences of the 2nd Battalion, the Manchester Regiment acting in this role for 2nd Division. Artillery was again reorganised as the presence of 25-pdrs was seen as essential; divisional artillery now comprised two field regiments of three batteries of 25-pdrs and one mountain regiment of three batteries of 3.7in. howitzers. The renewed use of anti-tank weapons in the Far East for bunker-busting meant that an anti-tank regiment of three batteries of 6-pdrs was reinstalled in the divisional set up. An Indian Army battalion in an infantry division in 1944 would comprise 866 men with A & MT of 12 jeeps and 52 mules, led by the troops of the Royal Indian Army Service Corps rather than infantry. This all meant that the new standardised division could now cover all the roles of the four previous, differently organised divisional structures.

The following section lists the combat records and organisational structures of the most important infantry divisions that fought in theatre. Space precludes a detailed treatment of every type of unit that served, and so a selection has been made of those that merit most attention.

British Army divisions

2nd Division

The 2nd Division was reformed after Dunkirk and made responsible for home defence on the Yorkshire coast. It then underwent training in late 1941 and embarked for the East in April 1942. The new commander was Major-General J.M.L. Grover. On arrival in India, the division undertook more training mainly at Ahmednagar, with some jungle warfare training at Belgaum and Combined Operations training near Bombay.

6th Infantry Brigade and the 1st Battalion Royal Scots took part in the First Arakan offensive. Originally the brigade was meant to take part in the amphibious

The British 2nd Division's formation badge. This badge was chosen in 1940 by the then GOC, Major-General H. Charles Lloyd. It is said to derive from the arms of the Archbishop of York and to be a reference to the time when Britain used to raise two armies, one being from the north. 2nd Division was a regular division at the outbreak of World War II and it formed part of the British Expeditionary Force in France and Belgium in 1940. It was transferred to India in June 1942 and went into action in Burma as part of the 14th Army in March 1944.

landings on Akyab Island, but when this was called off the brigade was brought in to aid numerous attacks on Donbaik. The brigade found itself the target of the Japanese counter-attack. However, lessons were learnt from the disastrous First Arakan, the first experience of jungle warfare for the British troops.

The whole 2nd Division was engaged at Kohima, crossing India and immediately entering action. The Kohima Garrison and 161st Indian Infantry Brigade were relieved by 2nd Division and went on to retake the surrounding areas: 4th Brigade advanced to the west of Kohima, 5th Brigade to the east, and 6th took the centre along with 161st and 33rd Indian Infantry brigades. By 16 May, Kohima had been recovered. This fitting epitaph was bestowed on the division for its role in the fighting there:

When you go home
Tell them of us and say
For your tomorrow
We gave our today

On 22 June, the 2nd Battalion, Durham Light Infantry together with A Squadron, 149 Regiment Royal Armoured Corps broke through the Japanese positions on the Kohima–Imphal road to join up with a company of 1/7th Dogras of 5th Indian Division. In July 1944 Major-General C.G.G. Nicholson took over command of the division, and after Kohima most of the division rested and retrained with the reinforcements. 4th Brigade continued to search out Japanese resistance at Ukhrul, and 5th Brigade with 23rd Indian Division pushed back Japanese forces into Burma and captured the village of Tamu.

The division was back in action in the fight from the Chindwin to Shwebo, which took 20 days. It then participated in the capture of Mandalay, by cutting off the escape routes for the fleeing Japanese. After the city had been captured, the division continued mopping up operations. The division was to be used in the capture of Rangoon but was not needed in the end. Indeed a large number of divisional personnel were eligible for home leave, having done the necessary three years and four months service under the Python scheme. The division was later earmarked for Operation Zipper, the recapture of Singapore.

Major-General Frank Festing (1902–76)
Major-General Frank Festing, Commander of 36th Division, is shown here driving his personal Willys MB on the road to Mawlu in November 1944. He led the advance into Mawlu when the leading platoon lieutenant was killed. He was nicknamed 'Front Line Frankie' because he believed in leading his troops from the front. Festing was educated at Winchester and joined the Rifle Brigade in 1921. He served as ADC to Major-General Sir John Burnett-Stuart, passed through Staff College in 1936 and was appointed Lieutenant-Colonel. Instructor at the Staff College in 1939. During World War II, he served as liaison officer to General Sir Bernard Paget in the raid on Trondheim in the Norwegian campaign. He was then given command of 2nd Battalion, East Lancashire Regiment and then command of 29th Brigade in October 1941. He led the brigade in Madagascar, capturing Diegon-Suarez, Majunga and Tamatove. He was promoted to major-general at the end of 1942 and given command of 36th Division. After World War II, Festing was appointed GOC Hong Kong and then posted back to London in 1946 as Director of Weapons and Development. In 1951 he was appointed Assistant Chief of Staff at SHAPE (Supreme Allied Powers in Europe) HQ. From 1952 to 1954 he was GOC British Troops in Egypt, then GOC Eastern Command, and in 1956 C-in-C FARELF (Far East Land Forces). He ended his army career as CIGS from 1958–61. (Photo: IWM SE 2524)

The formation badge of 18th Division. The windmill is a reference to the region of East Anglia, England, where the division was raised.

18th Division
18th Division arrived in Singapore in January 1942. It was originally destined for the Middle East but had been diverted to India, before being redirected to Singapore on Churchill's orders. The division had spent two months crossing the Atlantic and the Pacific before arriving in Singapore. It had been equipped for desert warfare and went straight into action with no training or chance to acclimatise. On 13 January a convoy arrived at Singapore carrying 53rd Brigade of 18th Division, along with anti-aircraft, anti-tank units and 51 crated Hurricanes. 53rd Brigade were immediately sent to Johore, where the Brigade took over 500 casualties and lost much of its equipment. They were able to re-equip but only at the expense of the newly arrived 54th and 55th brigades, and the Division's headquarters under

36th Division's formation badge. The badge was an amalgamation of the two individual brigade badges: the white circle for the 29th, after its first Commander General Oliver Leese, and the red for the 72nd.

Major-General M.B. Beckwith-Smith, who very briefly fought on Singapore Island. Most of the division spent the next four years in captivity.

36th Division

The 36th Division was raised from June 1942 as an Indian Army formation, consisting of 29th British Brigade and 72nd Indian Infantry Brigade. 29th Independent Brigade had been formed in June 1940. In 1941 Brigadier Festing took over its command from Brigadier Grover, later commander of 2nd Division. The brigade fought against the French in Madagascar and embarked for India in January 1943. In January Festing was promoted to command of 36th Division and was replaced as Brigade CO by Brigadier Hugh Stockwell. The 72nd Brigade was raised in England and commanded by Brigadier A.R. Aslett, who had captained the England rugby team before the war.

On 1 September 1944, the division was re-designated as British and on 14 December it received the 26th Indian Infantry Brigade as its third brigade, commanded by Brigadier M.B. Jennings. It took part in operations in the Arakan, re-capturing the tunnels on the Maungdaw–Buthidaung Road. The division moved to Shillong for rest before relocating to Ledo, where it came under the command of General Stilwell's Northern Combat Area Command. The division's first objective was to clear the Railway Corridor between Myitkyina and Katha on the Irrawaddy. The first action was at Hill 60 followed by Sahmaw, Thaikwagon, Pinbaw and Mawlu. 29th Brigade occupied Indaw and 72nd took Katha. The division covered about 200 miles and cleared the corridor in five and a half months; they were supplied by the 10th United States Army Air Force. It was the first formation to cross the Irrawaddy in January 1945 and advanced into the Shan States, coming under 14th Army Command. 26th Brigade took Myitson, where the Japanese used flamethrowers for the only time during the Burma campaign. It then took Mongmit on 9 March 1945. The division then moved to Mandalay and Maymyo by air and

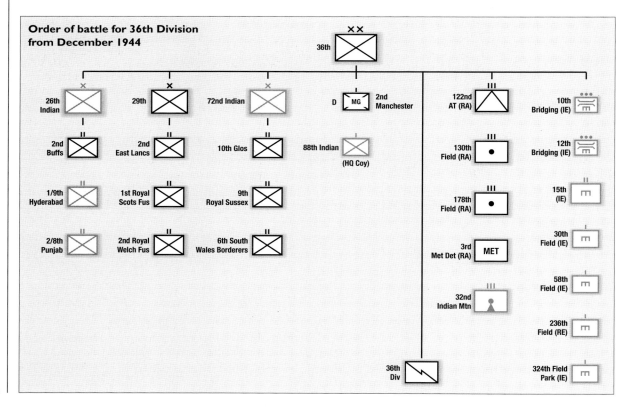

Order of battle for 36th Division from December 1944

road to relieve 19th Indian Division. It was then given orders to take Kalaw, although it was finally captured by 19th Indian Division. The 36th Division returned to India in June 1945; 26th Brigade was disbanded in September and the rest of the division was disbanded at Poona in March 1946.

Indian Army divisions

3rd Indian Division

The core element of 3rd Indian Division was formed at Jhansi as a Special Force of long-range penetration troops, after the First Chindit Expedition, on 18 September 1943. The first operation had featured 77th Indian Infantry Brigade, consisting of battalions of Burma Rifles, Gurkhas and the King's Liverpool Regiment who had been on internal security duties in India. During the operation, the railway lines were cut a number of times between Mandalay and Myitkyina. More importantly, the troops involved emerged from the jungle as heroic figures, lionised by the press as the first British and Commonwealth troops to get the better of the Japanese in the jungle, dispelling the myth of the Japanese 'supermen'. The operation bolstered morale in both Britain and India. However, only two thirds of the force made it back to India and of those only half were fit for duty again.

The division was made up of 77th and 111th brigades, three British brigades (14th, 16th and 23rd), and the 3rd West African Brigade. These were formed into groups of eight columns each and two wing HQs and a Force HQ. The force was designated as 3rd Indian Division on 1 February 1944. The division's role in 1944 was to support General Stilwell's forces 'behind the lines' in North Burma. Its second operation was launched in February and was supported by No. 1 Air Commando, US Army Air Force led by Colonel Philip Cochrane, who provided air artillery for the Chindits. The Divisional Commander was Major-General O.C. Wingate, who died in a plane crash on 24 March 1944. He was replaced by Brigadier Walter 'Joe' Lentaigne of 111th Brigade. It took three months for them to take the airfield at Myitkyina and another three months before the Japanese

Major-General Orde Wingate (1903–44)

In this photo, Brigadier Wingate sits in the passenger seat holding his staff on the way to HQ for a debriefing after the First Chindit Expedition. Wingate was born in India in 1903 and brought up in the Plymouth Brethren. He was educated at Charterhouse, entered the Royal Military Academy, Woolwich and was commissioned in the Royal Artillery in 1923. He served in the Sudan Defence Force from 1928–33. In 1936 he served on the intelligence staff in Palestine where he became committed to the Zionist cause. He organised and trained a force called Special Night Squads that proved very effective against the Arabs. He was awarded a DSO and a mention in dispatches for his work in Palestine and it was here that he came to the attention of General Wavell.

At the outbreak of World War II, Wingate was a brigade-major with an anti-aircraft unit. He was summoned to the Middle East by General Wavell, now C-in-C Middle East, to organise resistance in Abyssinia. In January 1941 Wingate crossed the frontier with the exiled Emperor Haile Selassie, and Gideon Force comprising Ethiopians, Sudanese and a small number of British officers and NCOs. His force successfully used guerrilla tactics, and entered Addis Ababa on 5 May. He was awarded a bar to the DSO for the Ethiopian campaign. However, Wingate had a temperamental character and on leave in Cairo he attempted suicide.

Wingate was again ordered by Wavell, now C-in-C India, to create a long-range penetration group to operate behind the lines in Japanese-occupied Burma. This new force was reliant on aerial supply and wireless contact. It was an extension of his experiences in Palestine and Ethiopia. His idea was to create a diversion of the enemy forces with regular infantry supported by air firepower, rather than stirring up resistance among the hill tribes, which remained a very secondary objective. After the first operation, Wingate's ideas developed to the use of strongholds. Wingate attended the Quebec Conference of August 1943 where his ideas were championed by Churchill. As a result he was promoted to Major-General and given the equivalent of a division. On 24 March 1944 he was killed when his plane crashed over North Assam. He is buried in Arlington cemetery, United States.

Wingate was a controversial figure and was often likened to T.E. Lawrence. In fact, he was distantly related to Lawrence. Wingate inspired loyalty and confidence amongst his Chindits but also came in for much criticism from others. (Photo: IWM IND 2194)

Order of battle for the 3rd Indian Division (the Chindits)

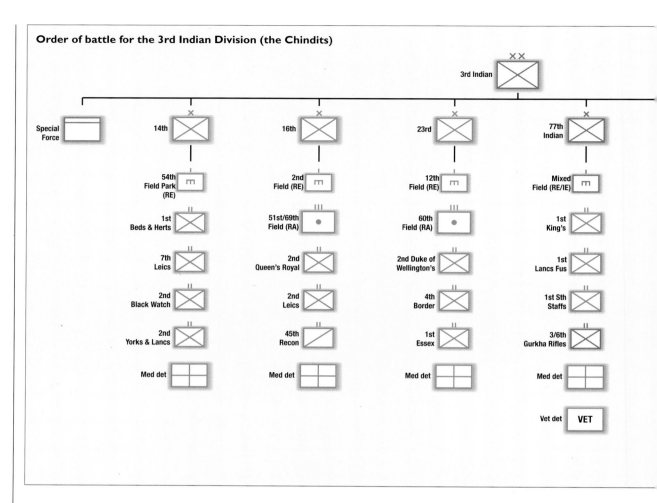

Special Force	14th	16th	23rd	77th Indian
	54th Field Park (RE)	2nd Field (RE)	12th Field (RE)	Mixed Field (RE/IE)
	1st Beds & Herts	51st/69th Field (RA)	60th Field (RA)	1st King's
	7th Leics	2nd Queen's Royal	2nd Duke of Wellington's	1st Lancs Fus
	2nd Black Watch	2nd Leics	4th Border	1st Sth Staffs
	2nd Yorks & Lancs	45th Recon	1st Essex	3/6th Gurkha Rifles
	Med det	Med det	Med det	Med det
				Vet det VET

The Burmese dragon on the 3rd Indian Division's badge was called a Chinthe; its job was to guard pagodas. The resulting nickname, Chindits, stemmed from the formation badge.

evacuated the town. The Chindits were involved in some of the hardest fighting in this operation, holding the strongholds of Aberdeen, Broadway, White City and later Blackpool against repeated Japanese attacks but also disrupting the enemy's supply lines. Lentaigne did not really share Wingate's vision and the Chindits were mostly used as infantry rather than as Long Range Penetration Groups under Stilwell's command. The division was disbanded on 31 March 1945.

5th Indian Division

5th Indian Division was formed at Secunderabad in June 1940 under the command of Major-General Lewis Heath. It was transferred to the Middle East in September consisting of only two brigades. The division was involved in many actions in the Middle East, most notably at the Battle of Keren, and in North Africa where it was involved in the defensive battles for El Alamein at Ruweisat Ridge. In May 1942 Major-General Harold Briggs took over divisional command and in October it returned to Iraq to undergo reorganisation as an armoured division with 7th Armoured Brigade. However, it was soon decided that the 'Fighting Fifth' would be relocated to the Far East theatre.

The 5th Indian Division started training in June at Chas in Bihar, and then moved to Lohardya, Ranchi, where it reorganised and retrained for fighting in the jungles of Burma. The division was already battle-hardened from its experiences in the Western Desert, but had to adapt to jungle warfare conditions. The amount of motor transport was reduced and animal transport introduced. The 28th Field Regiment was converted to a Jungle Field Regiment

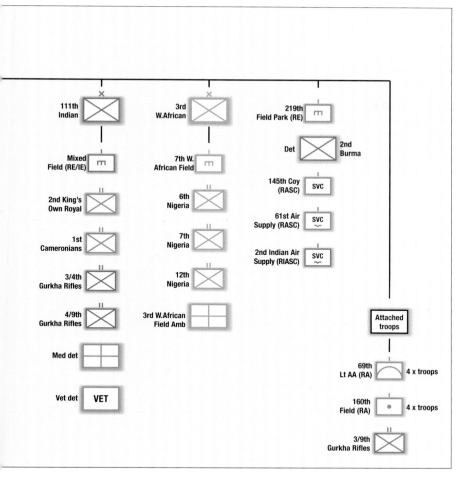

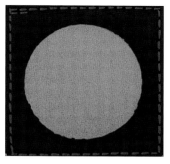

5th Indian Division's formation badge was nicknamed the 'ball of fire', among other less polite names. It derived from the red circles that were hurriedly painted on the division's vehicles when instructions were laid out that divisional signs must be displayed. The division had originally adopted the written Urdu figure 'five' (a heart-shaped figure) on a black background, but this was later changed for security reasons. The division was one of the few to fight the Italians, the Germans and the Japanese.

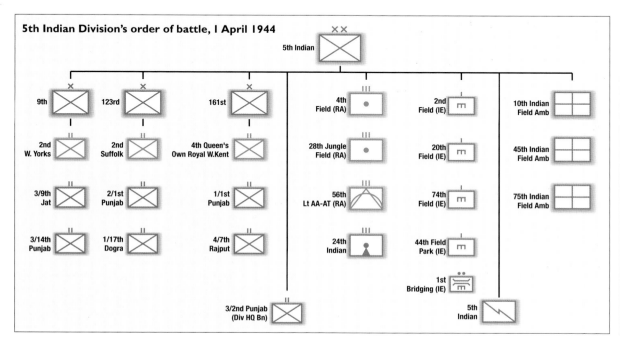

ABOVE LEFT Major-General Harold Briggs (1894–52) was Divisional Commander of 5th Indian Division from May 1942 until July 1944. After the war, he was Director of Operations in Malaya, 1950–51 and was responsible for the Briggs Plan.

ABOVE RIGHT Major-General D.F.W. Warren was brigade commander of 161st Indian Infantry Brigade in the Arakan and at Kohima. His nicknames included 'Bunny', 'Daddy' and 'Freddie'. He was a popular commander of 5th Indian Division from September 1944 but was killed when his plane went down on the way to Kalemyo, on 11 February 1945.

with 25-pdrs replaced by 3.7in. howitzers and 3in. mortars. The division also acquired jungle-experienced units such as the 27th Mountain Regiment, which had spent the last five months in the Arakan, and the 123rd Indian Infantry Brigade, which included the 2/1st Punjabis and 1/17th Dogras, which had both fought in the First Arakan. These veterans of the First Arakan helped educate the division in jungle warfare. The new brigade commander of the 161st Indian Infantry Brigade was Brigadier D.F.W. 'Bunny' Warren, who had been GSO1 14th Indian Division. Training was undertaken in co-operation with air support and tanks, which together with patrolling was seen as key to jungle warfare tactics.

Both the 5th and 7th Indian divisions underwent training in co-operation with the Royal Air Force for air supply. Both divisions were the first properly-trained formations of the Indian Army to fight in the Far East, in the Second Arakan campaign. They formed 15th Indian Corps, under the command of Lieutenant-General A.F.P. Christison, and were earmarked for the retaking of the Maungdaw–Buthedaung tunnel road. They relieved 26th Indian Division in late 1943. The plan was for 5th Indian Division to advance down the western side of the Mayu Range with Razibil fortress as its objective, while 7th Indian Division moved down the eastern side towards Buthedaung. The divisions were supported by the Lee tanks of the 25th Dragoons, while 81st West African Division covered their flank by advancing into the Kaladin valley to capture Kyauktaw.

In contrast to the First Arakan, the divisions were allowed time to acclimatise themselves to jungle warfare and gain confidence in the jungle through patrolling. The size and scope of the fighting gradually increased with actions at brigade level, when the Commonwealth forces had overwhelming superiority of numbers over the enemy. For instance, the 5th Indian Division's first major action was a direct attack on Razabil, made by 161st Indian Infantry Brigade, supported by bombers, dive-bombers and tanks. It was a failure, as the Japanese defenders were heavily entrenched, but the division quickly learned about the combat use of hooks, encirclement and tank support in their attacks. These tactics had been taught during training and for the first time were put into practice. Although unsuccessful, the experience gained helped shift them one step closer to defeating the Japanese in the jungle.

9th Brigade, commanded by Brigadier Evans, helped to relieve 7th Indian Division at the Battle of the Admin Box, whilst the rest of the division retook the Ngakydauk Pass. The second attack on Razibil on 12 March was more successful. During this operation 161st Brigade hooked around the fortress and cut off the enemy's lines of communication, while 123rd Brigade simulated a frontal attack in combination with an artillery bombardment. 9th Brigade was in reserve. The enemy was caught unawares, but unfortunately the advantage was not pressed home and the Japanese slipped away during the night.

The division was then transferred by air to the Kohima–Imphal front and continued afterwards on the Tiddim Road; it saw continuous action for 14 months. The division was in action again for the Battle of Meiktila and was earmarked for Operation Zipper. It was involved in internal security duties in Singapore and Southern Malaya, then was transferred to Java, and began returning to India in April 1946.

7th Indian Division

The 7th Indian Division moved to Chhindwara in January 1943 and was one of the first formations to embark on jungle training. The training team attached to the division by GHQ was led by Lieutenant-Colonel Marindin, who had participated in the retreat from Burma, with jungle lore taught by Captain Edgar Peacock, a forestry officer from Burma. By March, formation training was underway. There were exercises in co-operation with artillery, mortars and medium machine guns, called 'Blitz' tactics. From May to September the division carried out training in co-operation with the artillery and the 25th Dragoons, Royal Armoured Corps.

Further action in the Arakan was delayed by a major Japanese offensive, Operation Ha-Go, whose objective was to draw Allied troops into the Arakan, creating a diversion for the main Japanese advance towards the Imphal Plain. The Japanese plan in the Arakan was for the 55th Japanese Division to outflank

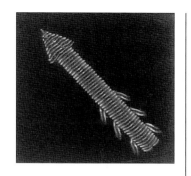

The formation badge of the 7th Indian Division, showing a gold arrow on a black cloth backing; as a result, it was also known as the 'Golden Arrow' division. The division was formed in Attock on the North-West Frontier on 1 October 1940, and its original badge featured a blue ball. The Divisional Commander, Major-General Frank Messervy, invested the arrow with the meaning: 'Forward to the target, straight and true, no withdrawal.'

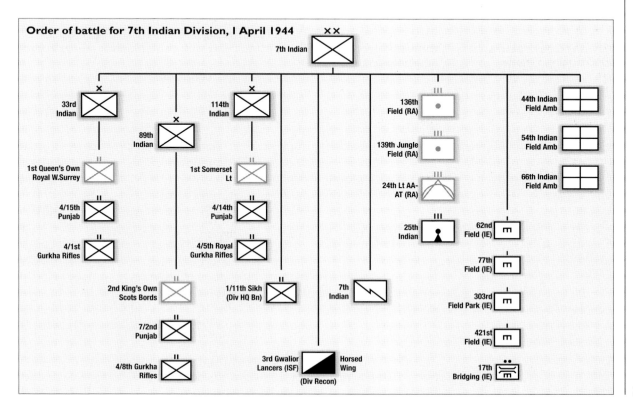

Order of battle for 7th Indian Division, 1 April 1944

31

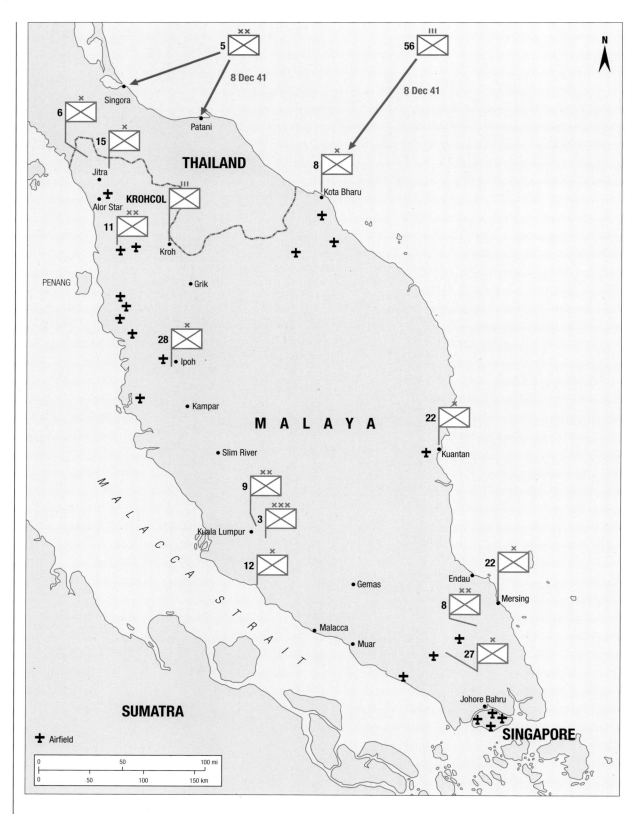

Malaya, with the dispositions of the British and Commonwealth formations, on 8 December 1941.

7th Indian Division and then split 7th and 5th Indian divisions apart, before destroying each in turn. The Japanese advance on 4 February 1944 was swift and Major-General Messervy's 7th Indian Divisional HQ at Launggyaung was overrun, causing a breakdown in communications. Brigadier Geoffrey Evans was ordered to defend the Administrative area of 7th Division at Sinzweya, later called the 'Admin Box'. This formed a refuge for Messervy and what remained of his HQ, who resumed command using wireless to contact his widely-dispersed troops. The defending troops prepared for all-round defence depending on air supply, and attacking the enemy positions and supply lines when possible. The avoidance of a disorganised withdrawal and the creation of an air-supplied defensive box was a feature learnt from the earlier campaigns and practiced during training.

The area chosen for the Admin Box was a flat, saucer-shaped area and thus was difficult to defend as it was surrounded by jungle-covered hills. At its centre was the highest position of 150ft called Ammunition Hill, with ammunition and ordnance at its base. By 10 February the Japanese had occupied most of the surrounding high ground, which dominated the Box. However, once the Japanese positions had been located by an observation post on Ammunition Hill, artillery with tank support brought overwhelming firepower down on them. This had the added advantage of destroying much of the jungle cover that would have facilitated future Japanese attacks.

In addition to the unfavourable defensive position, there was originally only one defending combatant unit, the 24th Light Anti-Aircraft and Anti-Tank Regiment. There was insufficient personnel to form a continuous line of defenders, and the defence had to rely on the counter-attacking abilities of newly arrived reinforcements, including two squadrons of the 25th Dragoons and a battalion of the West Yorkshire Regiment. On 7 February Messervy also ordered the 4/8th Gurkhas to come into the Box to take over the eastern gate and an important position called Point 315. This position had been previously undefended due to the lack of troops but was now seen as vital since it dominated the Box. The Gurkhas were attacked before they could reach their target and were initially forced back behind the perimeter, but a counter-attack by the 25th Dragoons, supported by the West Yorkshires, allowed them to take up their new position.

ABOVE RIGHT Major-General Frank Messervy took over command of 7th Indian Division from Major-General Corbett in July 1943. He had served with an Indian cavalry regiment, Hodson's Horse, during World War I. In World War II he had previously commanded Gazelle Force in Eritrea, 4th Indian Division and 7th Armoured Division (The Desert Rats) in the Western Desert and was well known for his escape from the Germans by impersonating an old soldier. He was nicknamed 'General Frank' by the soldiers of 7th Division. Messervy was made commander of IV Corps on 8 December 1944, and was later replaced by Major-General Geoffrey Evans. (IWM IND 3143)

ABOVE LEFT Major-General Geoffrey Evans (1901–87) was the Commanding Officer of 9th Indian Infantry Brigade during the Battle of Admin Box. He went on to command both the 5th and 7th Indian divisions.

The British used infantry and tank co-operation tactics, originally developed at Ranchi and refined at Razabil, in counter-attacks against the Japanese. On 12 February, Artillery Hill was subjected to a daylight attack by the Japanese. It was defended by the 24th AA-AT Regiment acting as infantry. The enemy hid in the jungle and took the position by surprise. A counter-attack by the West Yorkshires was unsuccessful, so two troops of 'C' Squadron, 25th Dragoons, were deployed firing high-explosive shells to clear the jungle undergrowth. When the tanks were at a reasonably close distance, solid shot was used to loosen the earth around Japanese bunkers and then high-explosive shells were used to destroy them. Finally, when the tanks were within a range of 100–300 yards, they fired their machine guns over the crest, allowing the infantry to advance without the threat of shell splinters. The infantry advanced to within 15 yards of the Japanese position before attacking with grenades and bayonets and capturing the hill. This action marked the beginning of the new techniques in tank and infantry co-operation and was in use for the remainder of the war.

Throughout its encirclement, the Admin Box was sustained by air supply. This was the first example of its large-scale use in the Burma campaign, with Dakotas successfully dropping food, ammunition and equipment. Not only was essential equipment dropped but mail and copies of *SEAC*, the paper of the Armed Forces in South-East Asia, were also delivered, which helped sustain morale.

The final Japanese attack on the Box came on 14 February. It was repulsed by the defending troops, and after this Japanese effectiveness rapidly declined due to the lack of supplies, since they had relied on capturing abandoned British supplies as in previous campaigns. The Box was eventually relieved on 27 February. According to Japanese sources the all-round fluid defence of the Box supported by air power could have been defeated only by overwhelming firepower, which the Japanese did not possess.

The Battle of the Admin Box and the defence of similar defensive boxes occupied by the remainder of the 5th and 7th Indian divisions heralded the

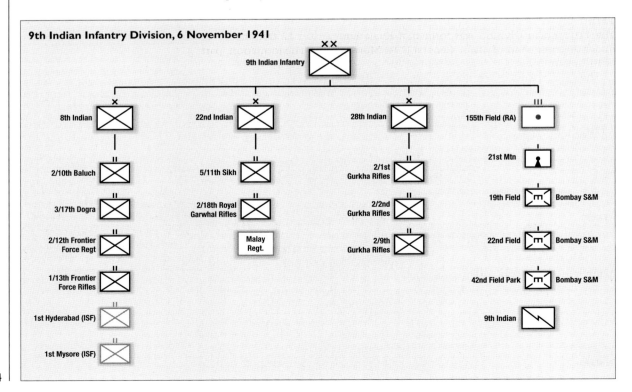

turning point of the Burma campaign. The myth of the Japanese superman was emphatically destroyed, and the events gave a huge boost to the morale of the 14th Army as well as to the civilian populations in India and Britain. Japanese tactics in the jungle had been effective up until this point, but the IJA had learnt nothing new. In the attack in the Arakan the IJA had relied on the Commonwealth forces retreating and leaving the supplies behind, and as a result they only had supplies for ten days.

The division also fought at Kohima and Imphal and in the pursuit to Ukhrul. It later advanced to Pauk and established a bridgehead over the Irrawaddy. The 7th were also involved in the last major battle in Burma, at Sittang, before disarming Japanese troops and evacuating prisoners of war in Siam.

The formation badge of 9th Indian Division.

9th Indian Division

The division was formed in Quetta in September 1940. It was sent to Malaya in March and April 1941. 8th and 22nd Indian Infantry brigades came under its command and it was responsible for the defence of the eastern coast of Malaya stretching from Kota Bharu to Kuantan. It was on Kuantan Airfield that Lieutenant-Colonel A.E. Cumming, commanding the 2nd Battalion, 12th Frontier Force Regiment won the Victoria Cross for conspicuous gallantry. During the withdrawal of the battalion and Brigade HQ, an enemy force attacked; Cumming and a small party of soldiers counter-attacked and held the enemy off until the whole party had become casualties and he had received two bayonet wounds in his stomach. Despite these wounds he drove in a carrier for more than an hour collecting the remnants of the battalion. He was wounded twice more and lost consciousness, but when the driver of the carrier tried to evacuate him, he recovered and insisted on remaining until he and the driver were the last survivors in the vicinity. After the surrender of Singapore, Brigadier Cumming led a small party of British and Indian officers through Japanese lines managing to evade capture and eventually reach Sumatra. The 9th Indian Division was broken up on arrival on Singapore Island on 31 January 1942.

11th Indian Division

The 11th Indian Division was formed at Kuala Lumpur on 12 October 1940, under the command of Major-General D.M. Murray-Lyon. The formation, part of III Indian Corps, was responsible for the defence of Northern Malaya.

The Japanese 25th Army invaded the Malayan mainland at Kota Bahru on 8 December 1941, with unopposed landings in Thailand at Singora and Patani.

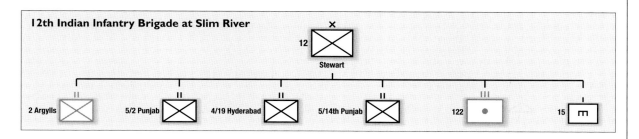

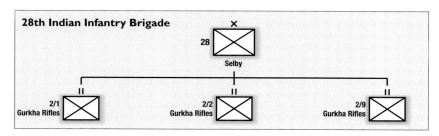

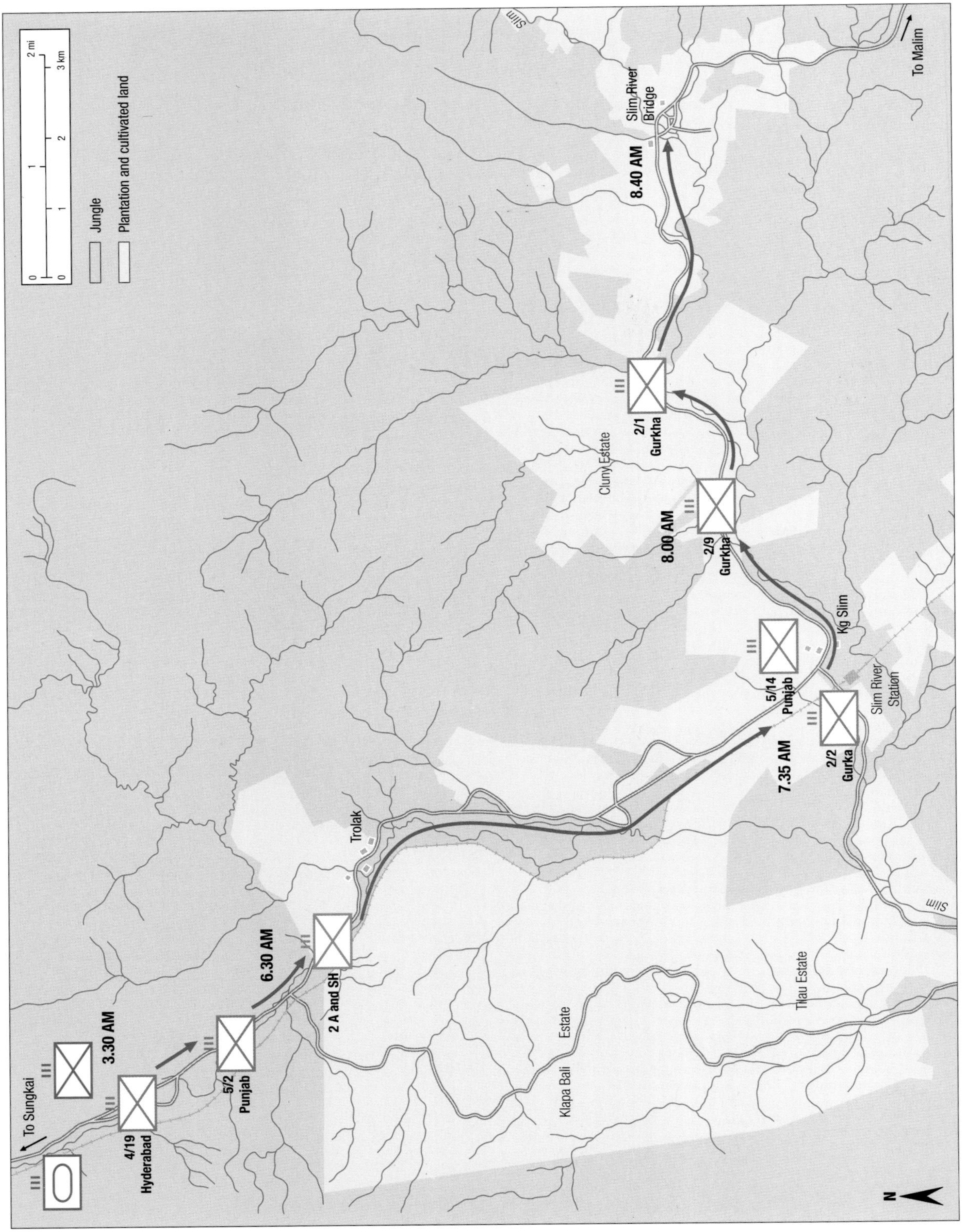
To Sungkai
3.30 AM
4/19 Hyderabad
5/2 Punjab
6.30 AM
2 A and SH
Trolak
Klapa Bali Estate
Tlau Estate
7.35 AM
2/2 Gurka
5/14 Punjab
Slim River Station
Kg Slim
8.00 AM
2/9 Gurkha
Cluny Estate
2/1 Gurkha
8.40 AM
Slim River Bridge
To Malim
Slim
Jungle
Plantation and cultivated land
0 1 2 mi
0 1 2 3 km
N

The Battle of Slim River, 7 January 1942. The Japanese armoured column's movements are shown in red, together with the time of arrival at key points.

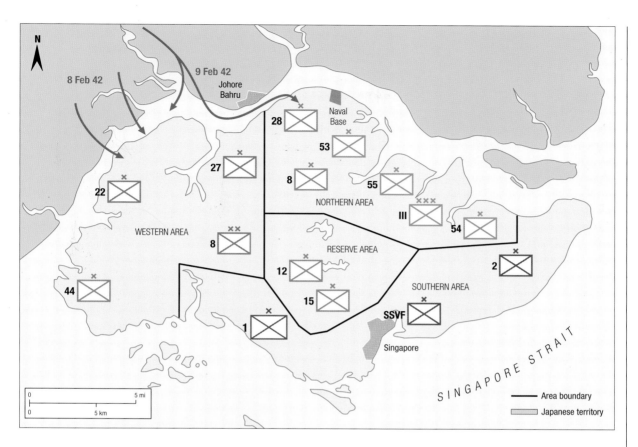

ABOVE Dispositions of the British and Commonwealth forces on Singapore Island, 8 February 1942.

The bridge and road over Slim River. It is still straightforward to tour the action at Slim River; the bridge at Trojak is still intact, and a sign for the Cluny Estate and the bridge over Slim River are clearly marked. The author recently undertook a battlefield tour using a map from the official history.

Order of Battle for 11th Indian Division, 1 November 1941

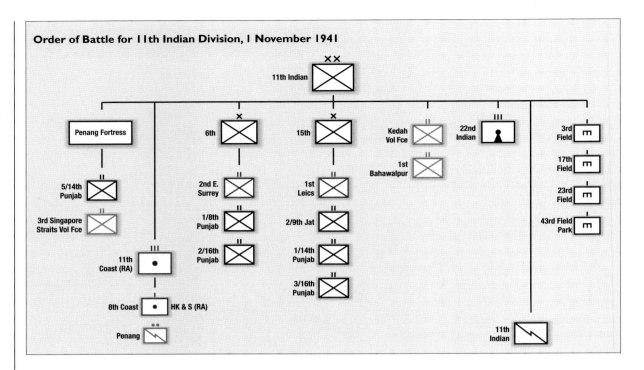

11th Indian Division's formation badge was still in use in captivity, on the entrance to Changi prison, with the motto added beneath of *Qui Ultime Melior Ridet* (he who laughs last, laughs best).

Operation Matador, a British pre-emptive plan to forestall the Japanese landings, was not ordered in time. The Japanese air forces quickly gained superiority over the obsolescent planes of the Royal Air Force and the Royal Australian Air Force. This, in addition to the sinking of HMS *Renown* and HMS *Repulse* on 9 December, meant that after three days the defence of Malaya and Singapore was the army's responsibility alone, without any significant support from the other two services. General Percival's plan for the army was for III Indian Corps under General Heath, comprising 9th and 11th Indian divisions with 28th Indian Infantry Brigade, to be stationed in the north and on the east coast of Malaya to forestall the Japanese forces and provide time for reinforcements to arrive in theatre from overseas.

The first major land engagement of the Malayan campaign was the Battle of Jitra on 11 December. The Japanese Army overran the fixed defences at Jitra in 14 hours using tanks, infiltration and encirclement, with demoralised defenders abandoning valuable equipment and supplies. These losses could not be made up and were particularly damaging as the division was the best equipped formation in Malaya. The fighting quickly revealed how badly organised, trained and equipped the division was for war in the jungle. Bewildered by the jungle and the Japanese, morale amongst the poorly trained Indian troops plummeted. In contrast, the confident battle hardened IJA appeared 'at home' in the jungle.

Some successful actions were fought by Commonwealth jungle-trained troops. The Argylls first action at the Battle of Grik Road on 19 December showed the importance of jungle training in Malaya. The Argylls defended in depth and undertook aggressive encircling patrols. When they took Sumpitan, the battalion had advanced 36 miles in five hours. It was noted that when the Japanese were attacked, they bunched together. When the Argylls finally had to withdraw due to the weight of Japanese forces, it was again a fighting withdrawal using ambushes and encirclement.

The division became so depleted due to the heavy losses sustained during the retreat from Northern Malaya that the division was forced to amalgamate four units to form two battalions. The 2/9th Jats and the 1/8th Punjabis became the

Jat/Punjab Battalion and on 22 December 1941 the 1st Battalion, Leicestershire Regiment and the 2nd East Surrey Regiment became the British Battalion.

The division was bolstered by the jungle-trained 12th and 28th Indian Infantry brigades at the Battle of Slim River on 7 January, but once again tanks were a decisive factor, and decimated both brigades. In this case, Lieutenant-Colonel Stewart, appointed to command 12th Indian Infantry Brigade on 24 December, did not employ the correct tactics; because of bad positioning and the lack of anti-tank weapons and mines, his exhausted and depleted brigade could not prevent the Japanese from smashing right through it. It should be noted, though, that the brigade had been in continuous action for three weeks. Stewart's tactics of filleting had been shown to be successful, but on this occasion their success had been demonstrated by the enemy. This defeat meant that the Japanese were able to take Kuala Lumpur unopposed. 11th Indian Division had been destroyed and General Wavell ordered Percival to bring the remnants back to Johore.

The Japanese reached Johore Bahru at the foot of the Malay peninsula on 31 January 1942. Fittingly, the last troops over the causeway were the pipers of the Argylls. The remaining uncommitted reinforcements on Singapore Island were 44th Indian Infantry Brigade, part of the recently formed 17th Indian Division; Indian and Australian reinforcements who had arrived between 22 and 24 January; and the rest of 18th Division, which had landed in late January. All these troops needed training (some even basic training) and they had no chance to acclimatise. They were nevertheless deployed in the front line of coastal defence. III Indian Corps took over the northern area; the Australians were on the west of the island with 44th Indian Infantry Brigade and the Singapore Fortress troops under Major-General Keith Simmons, consisting of the two Malaya Infantry brigades and the Singapore Straits Volunteer Force. The only reserve forces were the remnants of 12th and 15th Indian Infantry brigades.

Under heavy artillery cover, the Japanese attacked the Australian forces on 10 February and slowly advanced on the island. In the wake of a breakdown of communications, a shortage of water, fuel and ammunition, and general chaos, General Percival surrendered on 15 February. The defence of Singapore had lasted just 15 days, finally crumbling when the Japanese captured the water supply. The defeat was the worst in British military history.

14th Indian Division

14th Indian Division began training for jungle warfare in Eastern Bengal. On his arrival back in India after the retreat from Burma, Major A.D. Firth was ordered to establish and operate a Jungle Warfare School at Comilla for the division, together with Major Robin Parry. Its syllabus covered six key areas: the use of the 'hook' and outflanking movements; maintaining ground having been outflanked, in order to keep the initiative; useful minor tactics, such as ambushing; dispelling the myth of the impenetrable jungle; health discipline; and fitness.

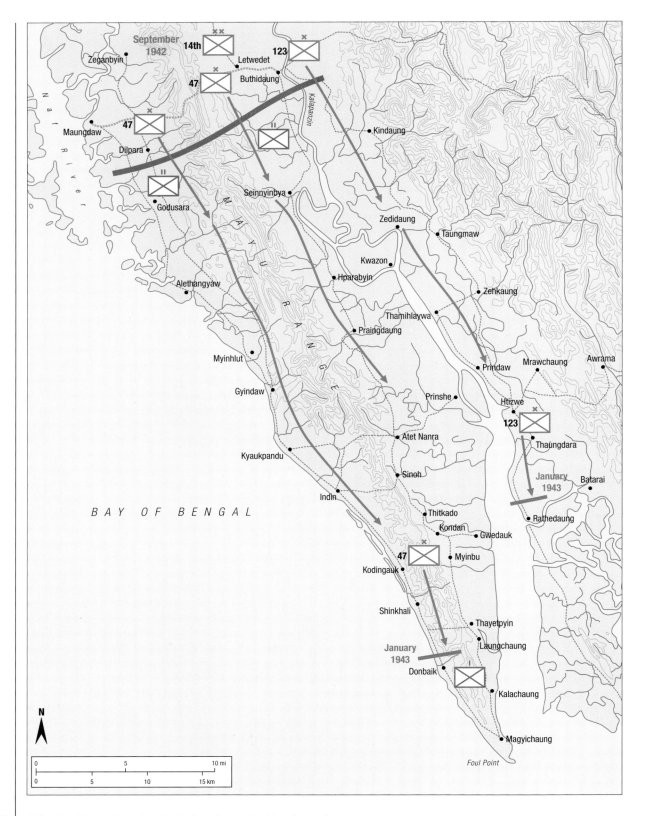

14th Indian Division's attack at 1st Arakan, clearing the Mayu Peninsula.

The cancellation of the amphibious 'Anakim' offensive to invade Burma and recapture Rangoon, prompted Wavell to mount a limited advance into the Arakan in late 1942. It initially involved 14th Indian Division clearing the Mayu Peninsula overland, whilst Akyab Island was captured by an amphibious attack mounted by the 29th Independent Brigade and 6th Brigade. The area chosen for the offensive consisted of a 90-mile long peninsula with the jungle-clad Mayu ridge along the centre, the Bay of Bengal on one side and the Mayu River on the other. The advance started on 21 September and a patrol of the 1/15th Punjabis quickly reached Buthidaung. Due to the lack of air cover, landing crew and the late arrival of 29th Independent Brigade, it was soon evident that the attack on Akyab would have to take place using only the 6th Brigade. The overland push by 14th Division was now the main part of the offensive, but progress was slow as the lines of communication needed considerable improvement.

The two Japanese battalions at the Maungdaw–Buthidaung line retreated with the build up of Indian forces, and thus the troops missed an opportunity of defeating a Japanese force. 47th Indian Infantry Brigade advanced down either side of the Mayu range and reached Donbaik in early January, whilst 123rd Indian Infantry Brigade headed for Rathedaung. The slow advance was not only dictated by the supply lines, but also the fear of exposing any flanks to the enemy. Unfortunately it also allowed time for enemy reinforcements to arrive.

14th Indian Division's formation badge. The division was raised at Quetta in May 1941 by Major-General H.H. Rich. The central peak represents Mount Takatu, which overlooks Quetta, itself represented by the Q-shaped border of the badge.

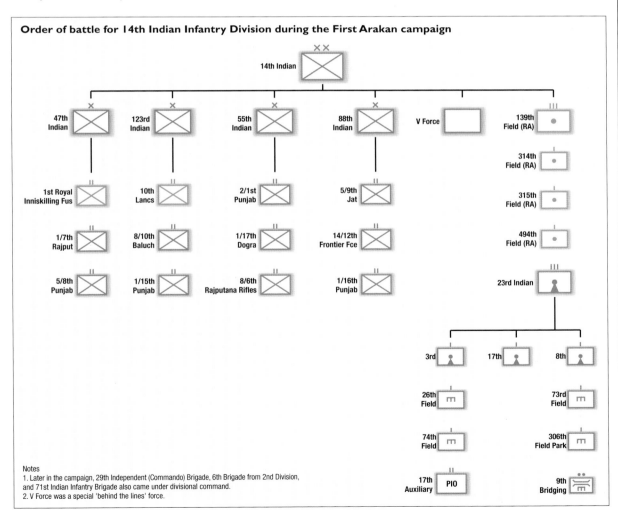

Order of battle for 14th Indian Infantry Division during the First Arakan campaign

Notes
1. Later in the campaign, 29th Independent (Commando) Brigade, 6th Brigade from 2nd Division, and 71st Indian Infantry Brigade also came under divisional command.
2. V Force was a special 'behind the lines' force.

On 7 January, a company of the 1st Royal Inniskilling Fusiliers reached Donbaik, now held by one Japanese company, and attacked the position unsuccessfully. Then the whole battalion, with field and mountain artillery, failed in another attempt over the next two days. Similarly, the 10th Lancashire Fusiliers and 1/15th Punjabis also failed in their attack on Rathedaung. A series of abortive attacks on both positions was made over the next two months with increasing strength. These were the first encounters with Japanese defensive bunkers.

On 18 January, two battalions attacked the fortified position at Donbaik and failed. 55th Indian Infantry Brigade relieved 47th Indian Infantry Brigade and on 1 February the whole formation, plus eight Valentine tanks, an additional one and a half batteries and a light anti-aircraft battery attacked the position. Once again the attack failed, partly as a result of the tanks having only arrived the night before with no training between the tanks and the infantry, and partly because three of the tanks ditched at the beginning of the assault. Artillery support was inadequate as neither rolling barrages nor smoke screens worked; the Japanese were too well dug in. There was, moreover, little co-operation between the two arms of service. Infantry attacks often started late and therefore did not take full advantage of the covering artillery fire, giving the Japanese time to man their fire positions to repel the attacks.

All attempts by 14th Indian Division to break the enemy defences had failed. The abortive attacks on Donbaik and Rathedaung brought time for the Japanese to mount a counter-offensive. In stark contrast, the Japanese managed to clear the Kaladan Valley and both the east and west flanks of the Mayu range; combined with encircling attacks on Rathedaung and Donbaik, all within a month, this pushed back the numerically superior Commonwealth troops in demoralising confusion. By March morale was generally low, with some units such as the 1/15th Punjab Regiment and the Lancashire Fusiliers having been in continuous action for five months.

In June 1943, 14th Indian Division was re-designated as a training division as part of the reforms recommended by the Infantry Committee. The division was based at Chhindwara in modern-day Madhya Pradesh. It was surrounded by jungle and the climate was comparatively mild, which meant that training could continue all year round. All arms, not just infantry, underwent jungle training, as it was such an alien environment to every soldier: British gunners, engineers and signallers were all trained at Chhindwara. The emphasis was on individual and section training for the infantry, whereas the other arms concentrated on weapons training. Recruits, including officers and NCOs, were trained at section and platoon level by a representative training battalion from their regiment within the two training divisions. This was an extension of the Indian Army practice of using training battalions in a regiment but for a specific terrain and type of warfare. The regimental training battalions had been instituted in 1921 as a permanent depot with one training company for each of the battalions in the regiment.

The division was commanded by Major-General 'Tiger' Curtis, who had served in both the retreat from Burma and the First Arakan. Only a handful of officers in the division had battle experience against the Japanese. Some instructors were sent from serving battalions, but units rarely sent their best men and, as it took three months to train the instructors, they were not the 'finished article' by the time the first intake arrived.

Training was intensive, for nine hours a day, six days a week, and often including three nights' work a week. Recruits spent the first month in the camp training in battle drill, field movement and weapons training. Range safety was lessoned, though no accidents resulted and this helped to achieve realism. Similarly, in order to match the Japanese efficiency with the mortar, units were trained to concentrate their fire. The second month involved training in the jungle, making and living in *bashas* (shelters made out of bamboo), with numerous exercises using live ammunition. One exercise that helped introduce the troops to the noise of battle and accustom them to the supporting arms involved troops advancing 250 yards towards an enemy held *nullah*. Artillery support came from 25-pdrs with medium machine-gun fire from the flanks. Once they had reached the enemy lines explosive charges were set off to simulate enemy artillery and support for a counter-attack. In all the exercises, there was strict discipline. Silence was maintained at all times, no litter was dropped and all ranks were stripped to the waist to aid acclimatisation, earning the division the nickname 'The Bareback Division'. There were long patrols of between 36 and 48 hours and leaders were responsible for their troops' administrative needs and anti-malarial discipline. Jitter parties were organised using likely Japanese ruses. Swimming lessons were encouraged as few Indians, and even fewer Gurkhas, could swim. At the end of the two months, the trainees were expected to march 25 miles a day with full equipment.

There were visits from serving officers to lecture on operational lessons from Burma and other specialists such as Jim Corbett, an expert in tracking and killing man-eating tigers in the Indian jungles. He was made a lieutenant-colonel with a commission to instruct jungle lore to the men of both training divisions. His book *Man-Eaters of Kumaon* was recommended reading in the training division and was translated into Roman Urdu by GHQ India. It described some of Corbett's experiences of tracking down tigers in the jungle. It was thought that valuable lessons of jungle lore could be learnt and then applied to operations against the Japanese.

The division had started taking recruits by the beginning of December 1943. 14th Indian Division made an important contribution to the ultimate defeat of the Japanese in Burma; the 16th (Training) Battalion the Punjab Regiment, part of 55th Infantry Brigade within the division, sent 1,957 trained soldiers to the 1st, 2nd, 3rd, 5th, 14th and 15th battalions of the regiment.

David Tennant 'Punch' Cowan (1896–1983), commander of 17th Indian Division between 2 March 1942 and 22 June 1945. Cowan was Deputy DMT at GHQ India in 1941 and then DMT, until taking up the post of divisional commander.

17th Indian Division

The 17th Indian Division was raised at Ahmednagar in June 1941. It was originally earmarked for the Middle East and began training at Dhond. The division's standard of general training was low, even before it was sent to Burma. In December 1941, Brigadier 'Punch' Cowan, officiating as Director of Military Training (DMT), had agreed with the divisional commander, Major-General Sir John Smyth VC, that the division needed a further six weeks' training once it had arrived in Iraq, where it was originally destined. Two of its brigades, the 44th and 45th, were nevertheless sent to Malaya as the military situation deteriorated. Thus, all that was sent to Burma of the original division was one brigade (the 46th) and the Divisional HQ. The little specialised instruction it had undertaken was confined to mechanised desert warfare, which was unsuitable for fighting in Burma. Although 17th Indian Division was strengthened after war broke out by the attachment of 16th and 48th brigades, and 2nd Burma Brigade, very little jungle training had been undertaken by the incoming troops and the formation was not a fully integrated fighting force.

On 20 January 1942 the Japanese 15th Army, comprising 33rd and 55th divisions, invaded Burma. As in Malaya, the Japanese seized and maintained the

The original 17th Indian Division formation badge featured a streak of lightning, but after the Japanese radio propagandist, Tokyo Rose, had called it 'the division whose sign is a yellow streak', and it had been driven out of Burma, the 'lucky' black cat was adopted. The adoption took place in 1943.

initiative in the jungle, particularly as the Commonwealth troops were equipped with motor transport and therefore were tied to the roads and continually out-flanked in the jungle. The GOC Burma, Lieutenant-General Thomas Hutton, wanted to keep the enemy as far away from Rangoon as possible, and chose a strategy of small pockets of defensive troops rather than concentrating his forces. The defending force was 16th Indian Infantry Brigade based at Kawkareik. The formation had now undergone some jungle warfare training but this was half-hearted as there was little direction on the subject. The Japanese pushed the brigade back from the Dawnas to Kawlareik in less than 48 hours and the defending troops were in disarray. The Japanese went on to infiltrate the Moulmein area and put in an unsuccessful attack on the morning of 30 January. Another attack in the afternoon was also repulsed, but the 7th Burma Rifles collapsed and the combined pressure of the Japanese attack and infiltration meant that a withdrawal was inevitable.

In addition, the unreliability of the Burma Rifles was a huge source of concern. The divisional commander, Major-General Smyth, wanted to use them in their usual role of irregular troops and for reconnaissance. However, this was deemed to undermine the prestige of the Burma Rifles. Instead, the Burma Rifles battalions fought as regular units, and fought poorly as a result. The Japanese seized the initiative in these early stages of the campaign forcing the British to retreat from a series of positions back towards Rangoon, despite pleas from High Command to mount a forward defence.

The bridge over the River Sittang was of vital importance to both the Japanese and the Allies; it was only 100 miles from Rangoon, and was a vital supply link both for the Burma Road to China and for reinforcements and

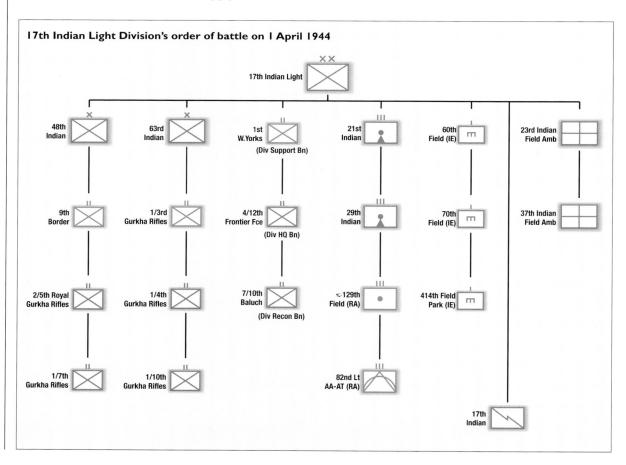

17th Indian Light Division's order of battle on 1 April 1944

supplies for the Burma campaign. Generals Wavell and Hutton thought it best to keep as much distance between the enemy and Rangoon. As a result Smyth was refused permission to withdraw early to the bridge to build up a defensive position to the west, which was unfortunate since the ground was suitable for open warfare, and the 17th Indian Division had been trained in this. Thus, when the troops did retreat to the Sittang Bridge, there was no time to create a defensive position and the Japanese were able to cut in behind the main body of the division. Although the bridge was held for as long as possible by units of the 48th Indian Brigade, the decision to blow the bridge before all the Allied forces were across was taken by the brigade commander, Brigadier Noel Hugh-Jones; this was done in consultation with Smyth, who knew that his other two brigades were still fighting on the wrong side of the bridge. Most of the Gurkhas, unlike the British, could not swim, so there were large numbers of Gurkha casualties, with many taken prisoner by the Japanese. The Sittang Bridge disaster sealed the fate of the defending forces. The 17th Division was reduced to 1,420 rifles, 56 Bren guns and 68 Thompson sub-machine guns. The division had to be reorganised after Sittang with some battalions amalgamating. Major-General D.T. 'Punch' Cowan took over command of the division on 2 March 1942.

The defence of Rangoon was now unfeasible due to the lack of troops and equipment. The army in Burma received further reinforcements, but they were mainly untrained. The exception was the battle hardened and well-equipped 7th Armoured Brigade, which arrived fresh from the Western Desert to shore up the defences. Little alternative now remained other than retreating northwards to Mandalay. On 16 March, General 'Bill' Slim was appointed corps commander of Burcorps, and realised that his troops were ill-trained and ill-equipped for jungle warfare. He made an immediate impact on the officers under his command, noting that the ideas of the staff were not necessarily correct.

The division covered the retreat from the Fall of Rangoon to the borders of India. There were successful actions, such as that of 48th Brigade at Kokkogawa on 12 April which resulted in a significant reverse. The brigade commander, Brigadier Ronnie Cameron, had realised the importance of all-round defence in the jungle, and with artillery and tank support from 7th Armoured Brigade repelled the Japanese attacks for two days, allowing 1st Burma Division to escape out of the Yenangyaung trap. This showed that an efficient and well-trained formation could adapt to jungle warfare even after being in almost continuous action for months. The Army in Burma had no real chance of stopping the Japanese and suffered a string of defeats at the battles of Yenangyaung, Monywa and Shwegyin. The British and Commonwealth forces successfully withdrew to India when it became clear that no other alternative remained. It was the longest retreat in British military history.

The officers of 17th Indian Division realised that they had to learn from their recent experiences in Burma. Training was of vital importance for the new recruits that were drafted into the division. The importance of silence, learning to swim, patrolling and getting used to the jungle were emphasised. As the first divisional training instruction noted in June 1942, the training had to be realistic. A second training instruction, issued the same month, stated that there was enough jungle training literature (including the division's own Cameron Report), and the division just had to 'get on with it'. The division reorganised as a light division on a jeep and pack basis.

The division fought at Imphal, took Meiktila and held it against heavy counter-attacks, and then embarked on the road to Rangoon to be present at the retaking of the city. The division covered 725 miles in three months and accounted for 10,263 enemy killed, 167 captured, 212 guns and 15 tanks destroyed. It fought longer against the Japanese than any other division and was often referred to by its troops as 'God's Own Division'.

General 'Bill' Slim driven by Major-General 'Pete' Rees, flanked by the troops of 19th Indian Division in Mandalay. Behind them in the jeep is Lieutenant-General Montagu Stopford, commander of XXXIII Indian Corps. (IWM SE 3530)

19th Indian Division

The 19th Indian Division was formed at Secunderabad on 1 October 1941, and along with 25th Indian Division defended Southern India in 1942. It underwent jungle training at Coimbatore, which was completed by December 1943.

The first major action executed by the division was at the Battle of the Irrawaddy Crossing. This was part of Operation Extended Capital, the revised Operation Capital, whose aim was to destroy the Japanese army in Burma. The

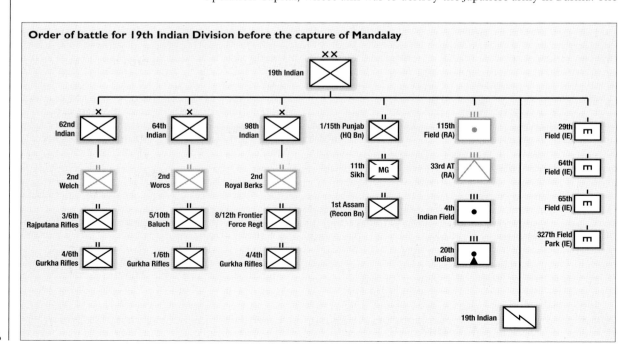

Order of battle for 19th Indian Division before the capture of Mandalay

plan was for XXXIII Corps and 19th Indian Division to cross the Irrawaddy, north of Mandalay and then move towards the city. This diversion would give the impression to the Japanese army that IV Corps was still in the north and XXXIII Corps in the south. The rest of XXXIII Corps, namely 2nd British Division and 20th Indian Division, would cross at Ngazin and the whole corps would encircle Mandalay. The Japanese forces would then engage the bulk of their forces in the defence of Mandalay, whilst IV Corps would move south, cross at Nyaungu, and advance for Meiktila. This would give the major battle that the 'manoeuvrist' General Slim desired.

On 9 January 1944 men of the 2nd Battalion, the Welch Regiment were sent across the Irrawaddy at Thabeikkyn for reconnaissance. The division then crossed at Kyaukmyaung (46 miles north of Mandalay) using rubber assault boats. Two regiments from the division also established a bridgehead at Thabenkkyin, 20 miles to the north, as a diversion, making the enemy think that the northern bridgehead was to link up with 36th Division. Both bridgeheads were held against repeated Japanese counter-attacks for 20 days, and contained Japanese troops caught on the eastern side of the river, particularly at Kabwet. The troops also took two tactical features inland – Minbaung Taung ridge and Pear Hill – both of which were key observation posts.

After this initial success the divisional commander, Major-General 'Pete' Rees, drove the division straight for Mandalay down the Irrawaddy with the Shan mountains to the east, taking Tongyi and Madaya on the way. He then formed 'Stiletto Force' consisting of the Divisional Reconnaissance Battalion,

Major-General Thomas Wynford Rees (1898–1959)

Thomas Wynford Rees was born in Barry in 1898. He served with the 125th Napier's Rifles in Mesopotamia during World War I, where he was awarded a DSO and a Military Cross. He served in Waziristan in 1920, 1922–24 and 1936–38. From 1926–27 he was an instructor at the Royal Military College, Sandhurst and afterwards took up the post of private secretary to the Governor of Burma.

On the outbreak of World War II, Rees was commanding the 3/6th Rajputana Rifles. He commanded 10th Indian Division for a short period before taking the command of 19th Indian Division in October 1942. To this division he was known as 'Pete', to the Welsh troops in the division 'the Docker', to the Indian troops 'General Sahib Bahadur' and to the 14th Army generally 'Napoleon'.

Rees later commanded the 4th Indian Division and then the Punjab Boundary Force which was charged with the task of policing the creation of Pakistan and an independent India. His last post, before retirement in 1948, was the Head of the Military Emergency Staff to the Emergency Committee of the Cabinet in Delhi.

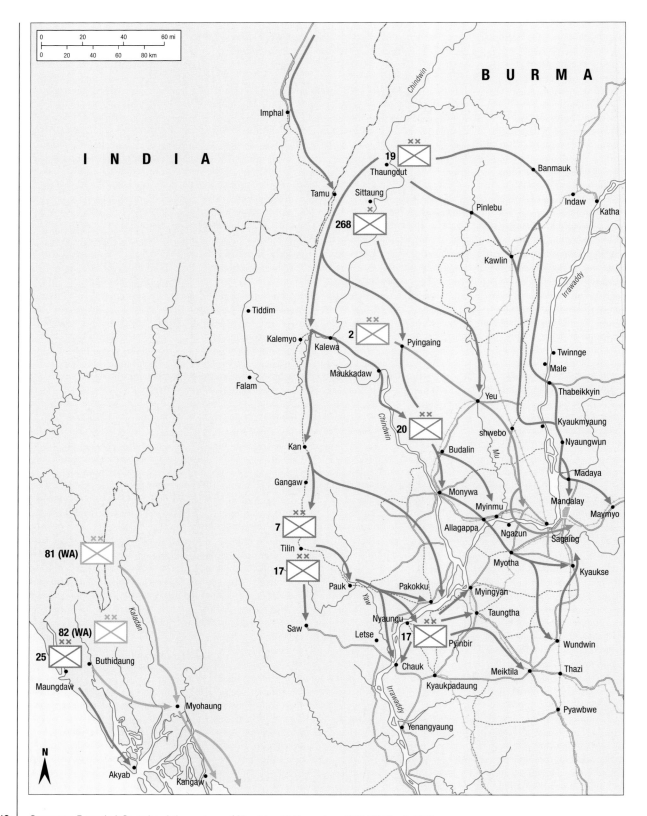

Operation Extended Capital and the capture of Mandalay, 19 December 1944–20 March 1945.

1/15th Punjab Regiment, along with British and Indian tanks, gunners and Madras Sappers. The force advanced along the side of the Irrawaddy and reached the north-west of Mandalay at 3 a.m. on 8 March, encountering little opposition along the way and surprising the Japanese defenders. The rest of the force came down the main road from Madaya, apart from a brigade, which took the hill station of Maymyo. After heavy fighting, Mandalay Hill and Fort Dufferin were taken on 20 March. Members of the division raised the Union Jack, the division flag and the regimental flag of the 1/15th Punjab Regiment on Fort Dufferin.

20th Indian Division

The 20th Indian Division was raised in Bangalore in March 1942. It was established and trained solely for the war in Burma. The GOC, Major-General Douglas Gracey, stationed in Ceylon, issued a training policy for his division in April 1942. It directed that all British officers, British other ranks, English-speaking Viceroy commissioned officers, and Indian other ranks should read the training pamphlets such as MTP No. 9 and *Japanese Tactical Methods*, the first training manual to deal with Japanese tactics and the defence against them, using examples from Malaya and the Philippines. *Japanese Tactical Methods* was first produced in Malaya in 1942 by Malaya Command. Gracey stressed the importance of reading the training pamphlets and using their ideas in training, and for them not to be regarded as 'just another bit of bumph'. In an appendix to his memorandum for training troops in jungle warfare against Japanese forces, Gracey encouraged the constant handling and use of weapons,

19th Indian Division's formation badge; as a result the division became known as the 'Dagger Division'. It was originally formed in India in 1941 under Major-General Sir John Smyth VC before he took over 17th Indian Division. The badge was designed and drawn by his wife, Frances. The dagger symbolised a readiness to strike against any attempted Japanese invasion in 1942.

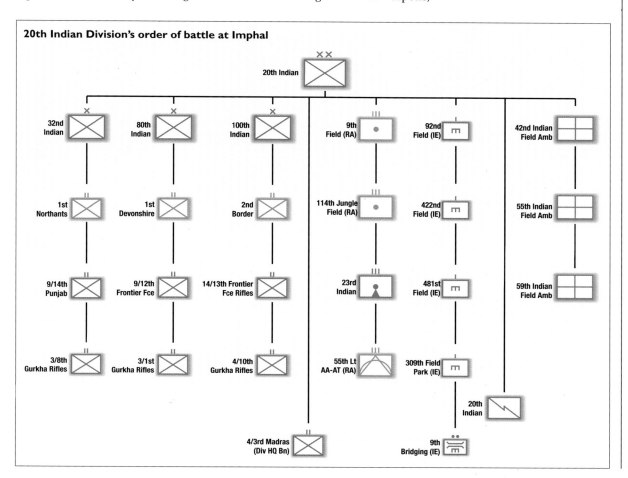

20th Indian Division's order of battle at Imphal

49

ABOVE LEFT Major-General
Douglas David Gracey (1894–1964),
commander of 20th Indian Division,
1942–46.

ABOVE RIGHT 20th Indian Division's
formation badge. According to Major-
General Douglas Gracey, the sword
stood for 'courage, chivalry, and
vengeance.'

Major-General Ouvry Lindfield
Roberts (1898–1986), commander
of the 23rd Indian Division, 1943–45,
during some of the toughest fighting
of the Burma campaign.

unorthodox tactics but strict discipline, and the use of booby traps and similar devices. Like other divisional commanders, Gracey wanted training to be realistic and undertaken by all soldiers in his division, including the Royal Indian Army Service Corps and the medical units. His training principles included: outflanking, encircling, attacking by day and night; counter-attack on the defensive; sparing use of ammunition; quick action against jitter parties; and flexibility off the roads. Soldiers were instructed to make the jungle their friend, travelling lightly and always staying alert.

The division saw action in Assam and Burma, where it fought on the Imphal Plain and crosssing the Chindwin and Irrawaddy rivers. It played a key role in the attack on Mandalay. Following its recapture of Magwe and the Burma oilfields, the division pursued the Japanese down the Irrawaddy valley to Rangoon. At the end of the war it was transferred to Indo-China to disarm Japanese troops, and was disbanded in March 1946.

23rd Indian Division

The division was raised at Jhansi on 1st January 1942 and was commanded by Major-General Reginald Savory. Most units joined the division at Ranchi and continued training at Lohargaga. Its main role for the next two years was patrolling on the Assam–Burma border, covering the retreat from Burma and later as a diversion for the First Chindit Operation. It was in reserve on the Imphal Plain until January 1944. By March, the division was dispersed with 1st Indian Infantry Brigade at Kuntaung, 49th Brigade at Ukrul and 37th Brigade training with 254th Tank Brigade and 50th Parachute Brigade. Both 37th and 49th then moved to the Tiddim Road to support the fighting withdrawal of 17th Indian Division. The 4/5th Maharatta Light Infantry of 49th Brigade stayed behind in the Ukrul area and fought in the very important delaying action at the Battle of Sangshak, alongside the 50th Parachute Brigade: the battalion suffered 260 killed, wounded and missing. The 23rd

Division fought in the battles for Shenam. In December the division underwent training for combined operations, as it was earmarked for Operation Zipper, and landed in Malaya after the surrender. It then transferred to Java in an internal security role and was heavily involved in fierce street fighting. It returned to Malaya and was disbanded in March 1947.

25th Indian Division

The 25th Indian Division was raised in Bangalore from August 1942. As part of Southern Army, the division's role was to defend Southern India against a possible Japanese invasion. It then undertook jungle training at Mysore, which was completed by December 1943. The division fought in the Third Arakan campaign. It was earmarked for Operation Zipper but left Madras after the surrender of Japan and accepted the surrender of the Japanese Army in Kuala Lumpar. The division was disbanded in Malaya in February and March 1946.

The formation badge of 23rd Indian Divison was conceived by the Divisional Commander, Major-General Reginald Savory, who later played a vital role as Director of Infantry. The red fighting cock was intended to be symbolic to both British and Indian Army troops while not alienating Hindu or Muslim troops. It was also meant to have a slightly bawdy interpretation. Savory said that frequently he had to insist that the result was 'a fighting cock, not a bloody rooster'. It was designed by Lieutenant-Colonel L.F.A. 'Busti' Maddocks.

Infantry of the 25th Indian Division scramble up one of the countless steep features of the Arakan.

RIGHT Major-General Henry Lowrie Davies (1898–1975), commander of 25th Indian Division from August 1942 to October 1944. He later joined the team of military historians who worked on the official history of World War II.

BELOW 25th Indian Division's formation badge, which prompted the nickname the 'Ace of Spades Division'.

BELOW 26th Indian Division's formation badge. It was called the 'Tiger Head' division after the Royal Bengal tiger stepping out of a triangle. The triangle represented the delta formed by the River Ganges; the division had been responsible for the defence of Calcutta in 1942.

26th Indian Division

The 26th Indian Division was raised at Barrackpore from March 1942 as the Calcutta Division. It fought in the First, Second and Third Arakan campaigns and in the recapture of Rangoon. During the disastrous First Arakan campaign in April 1943, with little jungle training and no time for acclimatisation, 26th Indian Division relieved the exhausted 14th Indian Division. Major-General Cyril Lomax then took over command of both divisions from the dismissed Major-General Lloyd. The division covered the retreat after the Japanese counter-attack. It was relieved in September by 7th Indian Division. In the Second Arakan it played more of a support role. On 21 January 1945 the division was tasked with the capture of Ramree Island to provide an air supply base for the 14th Army. It was a successful combined operations attack with the town secured 19 days later. The division was next involved in the occupation of Rangoon. It returned to India in June and was to be one of the divisions involved in Operation Zipper. Its role was changed to an internal security role for Siam, but as the situation worsened in the Dutch East Indies, two brigades were sent to Medan. It was disbanded in January 1947.

39th Indian Division

39th Indian Division was originally formed as 1st Burma Division ('Burdiv') in July 1941; in 1942 it was re-designated the 38th Light Indian Division. As there

Major-General Cyril Lomax (1893–1973), who commanded the 26th Indian Division from April 1943 to April 1945. He served with the Welch Regiment during the First World War and became Colonel of the Regiment 1949–1958.

was a Chinese 38th Division in theatre, after just one day it became the 39th Light Indian Division. It comprised two brigades, six mule and four jeep companies. It later became a training division in August 1943 and consisted of 106th, 113th and 115th Indian Infantry brigades. The 115th Brigade comprised the amalgamated 14th, 29th, 38th and 7/10th Gurkha battalions. For instance, the 38th Gurkha Rifles were made up from the 3rd and 8th Gurkha Rifles, under the command of Lieutenant-Colonel W.R.J. Spittle. Major S.C. Pickford was the training major for this new battalion, based in the Siwalik Hills. Despite having no previous experience of the jungle, a hurried attempt was made to learn before the first recruits arrived, by carrying out extensive patrols in the Siwalik Hills. Lessons learnt included the difficulty of marching to compass bearings and the importance of physical fitness. Pickford realised that once the jungle and the climate had been overcome, the Japanese would not present a problem. His training programme proved highly effective and was later adopted by the whole division.

The formation badge of 39th Indian Division.

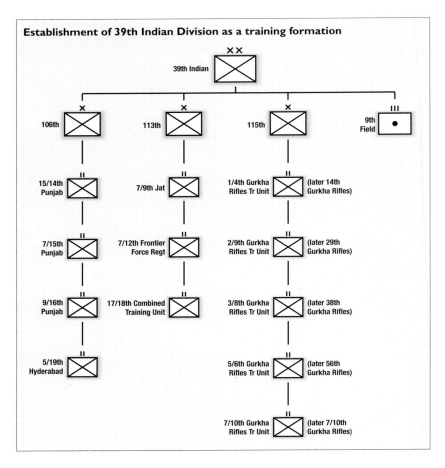

Establishment of 39th Indian Division as a training formation

39th Indian

| 106th | 113th | 115th | 9th Field |

106th:
- 15/14th Punjab
- 7/15th Punjab
- 9/16th Punjab
- 5/19th Hyderabad

113th:
- 7/9th Jat
- 7/12th Frontier Force Regt
- 17/18th Combined Training Unit

115th:
- 1/4th Gurkha Rifles Tr Unit (later 14th Gurkha Rifles)
- 2/9th Gurkha Rifles Tr Unit (later 29th Gurkha Rifles)
- 3/8th Gurkha Rifles Tr Unit (later 38th Gurkha Rifles)
- 5/6th Gurkha Rifles Tr Unit (later 56th Gurkha Rifles)
- 7/10th Gurkha Rifles Tr Unit (later 7/10th Gurkha Rifles)

44th Indian Airborne Division

As there was no need for an Indian Armoured Division in South-East Asia, 44th Armoured Division was disbanded in March 1944 and its HQ and divisional personnel were used to form 44th Indian Airborne Division in April. The establishment of the division was one air-landing brigade and two Indian parachute brigades each of one British, one Gurkha and one Indian battalion. A battalion group from 50th Indian Parachute Brigade dropped onto Elephant Point in the retaking of Rangoon on 1 May 1945. This was the only time Indian airborne troops fulfilled their airborne role.

The motif of Bellerophon astride a winged Pegasus on 44th Indian Airborne Division's formation badge was suggested by the novelist, Daphne du Maurier, who was married to Major-General F.A.M. 'Boy' Browning – the first divisional CO of 1st British Airborne Division. The motif was worn by 1st British Airborne Division and 6th Airborne Division, and was also adopted by 44th Indian Airborne Division.

8th Australian Division

The 8th Australian Division was formed on 1 August 1940, and was the only formation of Australian Military Forces used in South-east Asia. Originally it consisted of three brigades: the 22nd, 23rd and 27th. Major-General Gordon Bennett took over its command from General Sturdee on 24 September. Bennett was a very forceful character, often at odds with his fellow Australian generals, Malaya Command and even the brigadiers under his own command. He eventually secured a definite role for the Australian forces in Malaya with the Johore area coming under his command: 8th Division now comprised

22nd Brigade commanded by Brigadier Taylor, and 27th Brigade, which arrived on the 15th August under Brigadier Maxwell. Later, 45th Indian Infantry Brigade also came under its command.

The Australians of 8th Division also took more than a passing interest in jungle training. Brigadier H.B. Taylor of 22nd Brigade was posted ahead of his brigade to make a tour of all the British and Indian Army units in Malaya. He concluded that very few were advanced in training for jungle warfare except for the Argylls. Like most of the Indian formations, the Australian Division had trained for desert warfare.

The colour patch of 8th Australian Division Headquarters.

Both Taylor and Major-General Gordon Bennett, Divisional GOC, realised the importance of jungle training. Major C.G.W. Anderson, CO 2/19th Battalion, was made responsible for jungle training, since he had gained valuable experience whilst serving with the King's African Rifles in East Africa during World War I. Their doctrine was also partly based on the *Tactical Notes for Malaya*, which was reprinted in Australia, and was issued on arrival in Malaya.

The Australian action at Gemas on 14 January showed the importance of jungle training. 2/30th Battalion commanded by Brigadier Galleghan laid an ambush for the advancing Japanese forces. About 300 enemy soldiers on bicycles were allowed to pass the ambushing forces on the road to Gemas and go over the bridge at Sungei Gemencheh; however, when a further 700–800 came towards the position, the ambush was set off by an explosion on the bridge. Several hundred Japanese died, in contrast to 80 Australian casualties.

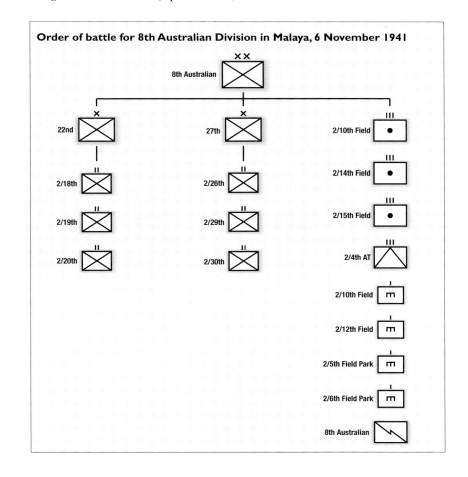

Order of battle for 8th Australian Division in Malaya, 6 November 1941

The formation badge of 11th East African Division. The double-horned rhino adopted by the division was only found in East Africa and in particular in Kenya and Tanganyika. When 21 (East African) Infantry Brigade arrived in Ceylon it featured a whole rhino on its badge motif, but had to abandon it as 1st Armoured Division's badge was very similar. Ceylon Army Command sanctioned the division's new badge on 23 August 1943.

This was the first part of the Australian learning curve in jungle warfare, which was steepened a year later by the Australian victory at Milne Bay in New Guinea. The remainder of the Johore defensive line was made up of the retreating 9th Indian Division, the newly arrived and un-acclimatised 53rd British Brigade of 18th Division, and the ill-trained 45th Indian Infantry Brigade. However, the Japanese also had reinforcements, namely the Imperial Guards divisions, who destroyed 45th Indian Infantry Brigade at Muar and forced the withdrawal to Singapore Island where the Australians took up position on the west of the island.

West and East African divisions

81st West African Division

The 81st West African Division was formed on 1 March 1943 in Southern Nigeria. It was the first division ever to be formed from units of the West African colonies of Nigeria, the Gold Coast, Sierra Leone and Gambia. 3rd Brigade was from Nigeria, 5th Brigade from the Gold Coast, and 6th Brigade was mixed with battalions from the Nigeria, Sierra Leone and Gambia.

The importance of collective jungle training was also appreciated outside India, as some jungle training was carried out in Africa prior to the movement of 81st West African Division to India and then Burma. For example, Captain Denis Arnold of the 7th Nigeria Regiment attended the West African Training School at Enugu for jungle training in 1942, before undergoing further training with the Chindits in India.[8] As Major-General Woolner commented in his divisional report, at this time there was no accepted jungle warfare doctrine or

---

8 See *Arnold Mss.*, Papers of Captain D. E. Arnold, IWM, 99/21/1.

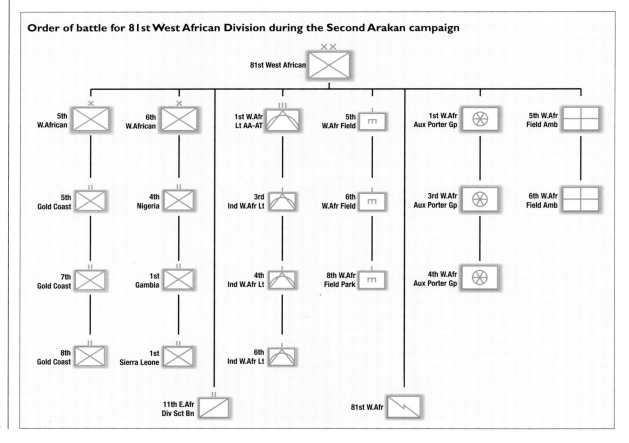

Order of battle for 81st West African Division during the Second Arakan campaign

even a training pamphlet. The Royal West African Frontier Force produced its own *Platoon Battle Drills and Jungle Tactics for the RWAFF* in September 1943, which encompassed internal security experience, as well as that of a more conventional nature learned during World War I. However, once again there was no central coordination for jungle training.

The division transferred to India in August 1943. Their jungle training had been similar to what was being taught in India, but due to the concentration on jungle warfare the formation had undergone little collective training, and none with formations in India before going into action. Woolner did read Wingate's report on the First Chindit Operation and found it very useful, as it was very similar to the role the division played in the Burma campaign; this was closely akin to that of the Chindits, as they fought a separate action in the campaign with air support from the RAF. Although they had no time for collective training before going into action, they captured Kyauktaw, but a Japanese counter-attack drove the division out of the Kaladin Valley in the Second Arakan campaign. They also fought successfully in the Third Arakan. Japanese prisoners taken in the Arakan told their interrogators that the West Africans were the 'best jungle fighters'. 3rd (West African) Brigade fought with the Chindits during Operation Thursday in 1944.

82nd West African Division

82nd West African Division was formed in Nigeria in August 1943 and dispatched to India in July 1944. There was little opportunity for jungle training in India. The division joined XV Corps in the Arakan in November 1944. Together with 81st West African Division, it took Myohaung on 25 January 1945. Major-General Hugh Stockwell was appointed as the Divisional Commander in January; his meteoric rise had taken him from major to major-general in less than five years. After Myohaung, the division was to advance towards Hpontha, with one brigade heading towards Kangaw and the other two for Kweguseik. The division reached Hpontha on 29 January, Kangaw was taken on the 28 February, and Kyweguseik was found unoccupied on 22 February. The division suffered the heaviest casualties in the corps, as it fought mostly at close-quarters in the jungle where it was difficult to provide artillery and air support.

11th East African Division

11th East African Division was raised in East Africa in May 1943. Three battalions were from Uganda and Nysasaland, two from Kenya and Tanganyika, and one

ABOVE LEFT The formation badge of 81st West African Division. The divisional commander, General Woolner, chose the black spider design, which represented Ananse, a figure in Ashanti mythology who could overcome his enemies through guile. The badge was worn head down so it would appear to be going forward when a soldier was about to fire his weapon. The spider was often mistaken for a tarantula, but these were not indigenous to West Africa.

ABOVE RIGHT 82nd West African Division's formation badge. It shows two spears crossed on a native carrier's headband and symbolised 'Through our carriers we fight'. This showed the important role the carriers played in the movement and supply of the division, even carrying 3.7in. howitzers. The yellow on black colouring was adopted to conform with that of 81st West African Division.

from Northern Rhodesia. The units had British officers and some British Warrant Officers and NCOs; it was commanded by Major-General C.C. Fowkes. The division was sent to Ceylon in June 1943 as part of the garrison but also underwent jungle training. The formation was moved to Chittagong and then on to Imphal, where it joined XXXIII Indian Corps. The corps' objective was to advance to the Chindwin with 5th Indian Division on the right flank and 11th East African Division advancing down the Kabaw Valley (called 'Death Valley' as it was disease ridden) with the aim of clearing it, reaching the Chindwin and linking up with 5th Indian Division at Kalemyo. This approach surprised the Japanese defenders as they were expecting an advance down the Tiddim Valley. The division fought in the Kabaw Valley from August 1944 onwards and managed to fight its way through the monsoon, reaching Shwegy in December. The soldiers of the 11th East African were also the first troops to cross the Chindwin.

Troops of the Royal Berkshire Regiment, 19th Indian Division, pass a dead Japanese soldier as they enter Madaya.

An ambulance convoy prepares to leave the 'Box' with wounded troops of 7th Indian Division at the end of the Battle of the Admin Box.

Tactics

From 1940, the Argyll and Sutherland Highlanders in Malaya underwent two years of jungle training, mainly because their brigade was to act as the mobile reserve in the event of an invasion and therefore had to acquire experience of the jungle. Major Ian Stewart believed that it took six months to get a battalion fully acclimatised to the jungle. He realised that control of the roads was vital and this would be best maintained through operating in the surrounding jungle rather than in static defence. He developed tactics consisting of what he termed 'filleting' and the use of 'tiger patrols', which were practised in training until the jungle became 'a friend and not an enemy' to the Argylls. 'Filleting' consisted of an encircling attack to the rear of the enemy combined with a frontal one that would split the enemy. 'Tiger patrols' involved five men going behind enemy lines, also encircling the enemy. They were not meant for reconnaissance but as attacking patrols that would sap the enemy's strength.

The Jungle Book's section on the infantry reiterated the importance of this arm as the most critical one in the jungle:

> Infantry is the paramount arm in the jungles owing to its comparative mobility, and well trained infantry can dominate the jungle. Special training, however, is necessary to accustom troops to jungle conditions and jungle life. This training must inculcate the ability to move quickly and silently; to find the way accurately and with confidence; to shoot straight and quickly at disappearing targets from all positions on the ground, out of trees and from the hip; to carry out tactical operations in

Troops of the Manchester Regiment cleaning their weapons. The soldier on the left is cleaning his 2in. mortar, while the other two in the foreground are cleaning a Mark 2 Bren gun and a Sten gun Mark 2. The soldier in the rear is cleaning his No. 2 Mark I Enfield revolver. (IWM SE 3758)

An example of attacking tactics. The reconnaissance patrols would be sent forward to determine the strength of the enemy. Then a feint of a small number of fighting patrols would attack on the right flank whilst the main body of the force would attack on the left and rear flanks.

Key:

 Allied troops

 Intended fire of Allied troops once in position

 Allied positions

 Japanese troops

 Allied position

 Allied troops

 Japanese troops

 Movement of Japanese troops

 Movement of Allied troops

the jungle by means of battle drills, known to all, and without waiting for detailed orders. Above all the highest pitch of physical toughness is essential in all ranks, particularly officers, and the leadership of junior commanders must be confident, offensive and inspiring.

It noted the need for thorough training for infantrymen in the use of rifles, bayonets, grenades, automatic weapons in the jungle:

> The feeling of loneliness and the bad visibility in the jungle tend to make men jumpy if they have not complete confidence in themselves. The highest standard of sub-unit and individual fire control is therefore necessary, and training must be directed to this end.[9]

Mortars were seen as essential, as often artillery support was not available or a position might be inaccessible. In these instances the infantry would need to rely on mortar support; the divisional artillery always allotted a proportion of mortar batteries for this purpose.

As in previous editions of MTP No. 9, there were sections on attack, active defence and ambushes. The section on patrolling had increased, while the chapter on withdrawal had been reduced to an emphatic: 'THERE WILL BE NO WITHDRAWAL'. There were also detailed sections on maintenance, detailing for example the scale of rations needed and supply details.

---

9 MTP No. 9, *The Jungle Book*, 4th edition, (September, 1943), p. 4.

An example of aggressive defensive tactics where the enemy is encountered advancing along a track. Troops would be sent out to pre-empt any enemy outflanking manoeuvres.

Key:

Allied troops

Recce patrol (3 men)

Allied positions

Japanese troops

Movement of Allied troops

Fighting patrol (9 or more men)

Patrolling

Patrolling was of vital importance in the jungle, and was divided into two types: reconnaissance and fighting. Reconnaissance was usually conducted by an NCO and six men, and its object was to gain intelligence without fighting the enemy. A fighting patrol was meant to obtain unit identification and other material by ambushing and attacking the enemy, and therefore usually consisted of about 30 men plus an officer. The fighting patrol was often organised into three manoeuvre sections and one support section, the latter armed with 2in. mortars, rifle grenades and two light machine guns. Troops were encouraged not to leave litter on patrol; movement was off the tracks so as not to give intelligence to the enemy; and an easily recognisable rendezvous was essential. Patrols were not to be deterred from their purpose, as *The Jungle Book* stated in capital letters: 'AN ENCOUNTER WITH THE ENEMY EN ROUTE MUST NEVER DETER A PATROL FROM COMPLETING ITS TASK.' [10]

In the attack

During an attack in the jungle, the attacker gained the advantage through intelligence and previous patrolling, and held the element of surprise. Thus, the frontal approach was usually discounted in favour of encirclement and flanking movements. The attacking force would be divided into four components. The first element fixed the track or some tactical feature and fixed the enemy. The second and third outflanked one or both of the enemy's flanks,

Ambushes could be used when patrolling, in attack, and in defence. This illustration from MTP No. 52 shows tactics for an ambush on a track when the direction of the enemy is not known. Ambush parties could be located on a track facing both ways to strike an enemy coming from either direction. Each, if not engaged, could assist the other by engaging the almost certain enemy outflanking movement. Mortars could be positioned in order to fire along the track at places where the enemy might halt. After the parties had withdrawn, the mortar could continue firing on the point of ambush as long as it had covering fire.

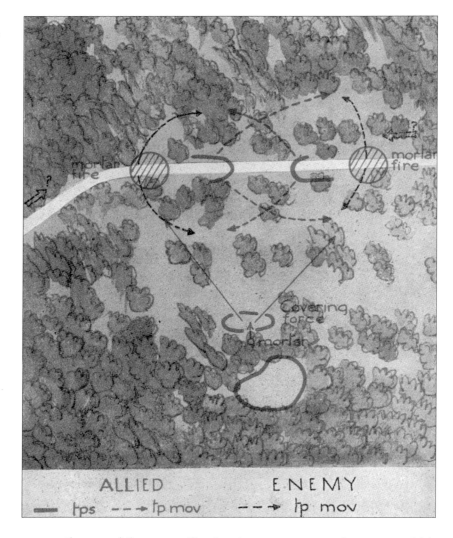

ALLIED
—— tps ——→ tp mov

ENEMY
——→ tp mov

or even the rear of the enemy. The fourth component was the reserve, which would exploit the success of the flanking movement or be able to contain the enemy counter-attack. Similar tactics had proved effective when used by the Japanese in their advance through Malaya and Burma. Troops needed to counter-attack immediately after Japanese infiltration before the enemy could build up its forces.

The major change in the final edition of *The Jungle Book* was a section suggesting how to counter the style of Japanese defence such as that seen in the Arakan. For example, for the infantry it suggested the employment of previously underused anti-tank weapons. Co-operation with the other arms was also essential in bunker busting. The artillery could provide barrage fire on a narrow front, and it was suggested that lifts of a hundred yards every three minutes were needed in average jungle, with a slower rate of fire in thicker jungle. It noted that aircraft and tanks could be of equal value in support of infantry. Aircraft were also used for reconnaissance, air supply as well air support.

The Japanese were equally determined in defence as in attack, with their use of the supporting defensive bunker system. In the First Arakan campaign, the bunkers at Donbaik were very difficult to destroy as they were skilfully sited, carefully camouflaged and strongly built, and seemed to be indestructible. Each normally consisted of a small heavily fortified post of about 10 men who were positioned to protect a neighbouring bunker. The two strongest bunkers at Donabik were named S4 and S5 and were linked by interconnecting positions. S5 was a hollowed-out mound on a dry watercourse, making it almost invisible to the attacking British forces. Shelling did inflict casualties on the bunker defenders, and as a result the Japanese left one sentry in the bunker while the rest of the platoon hid in nearby caves during the Allied bombardments. Once the shelling had ceased, the Japanese would occupy the bunker to repel the imminent attack. In fact, Allied tactics during the First Arakan seemed to be one-dimensional, consisting of artillery barrages followed by the infantry going forward. Even when a surprise attack was proposed, it was still preceded by an artillery barrage.

New tactics were needed to counteract these extremely strong Japanese defences. The infantry had to co-operate with other arms, such as artillery, tanks and air support, as well as maximise their own resources such as the PIAT (Projector Infantry Anti-Tank). A system was drawn up to destroy these defensive positions. First, a reconnaissance patrol would be sent out for intelligence. Then the bunker and the surrounding area would be bombarded by artillery, armour or air bombardment. The attack itself would consist of infantry supported by tanks, machine guns and 6-pdr anti-tank guns, which were also quite effective at bunker-busting. Movement was indicated by the leading infantry throwing down No. 77 smoke grenades every five or ten minutes; the supporting arms could thus adjust their fire. In addition, 25-pdrs, 3in. howitzers and 3in. mortars could fire smoke as well as high-explosive shells as the infantry approached the objective, giving them cover from the defences. Tanks, once at a reasonably close range, would use solid shot to loosen the Japanese bunkers, then switch to high-explosive shells to burst inside the bunkers. When the tanks were within 100 to 300 yards, they switched to machine-gun fire to allow the infantry to advance without the threat of shell splinters. The infantry would then advance to within 15 yards of a Japanese bunker before attacking with grenades and bayonets. The tanks could also help with the immediate enemy counter-attack, by changing to 75mm armour-piercing shells to give more support to the infantry and loosen the supports of the bunker before the enemy was able to return there. Finally, another wave of infantry was usually sent in to mop up and deal with the counter-attack.

In the defence

New tactics were also needed in defence, since it was impossible for a static defensive line to fend off a jungle attack. The actual defensive position was ideally a series of mutually supporting posts, which in the jungle could be quite close together. Automatic weapons were essential for this mutual support because artillery was not always available. The posts also had to be self-contained, with sufficient water and supplies for several days, and had to make the most of the available natural obstacles and camouflage. In addition, posts could be defended by ground and tree snipers. Snipers, patrols and listening posts combined would help prevent enemy infiltration, but also essential was a central reserve, ready to counter-attack immediately. The most important element in defence was aggression.

This diagram from MTP No. 52 shows how to destroy enemy sniper positions. Enemy snipers could be encouraged to encroach into a set area by a lack of patrolling for a few nights. The area could then be cleared up by intensive anti-sniper patrols, as shown in this diagram.

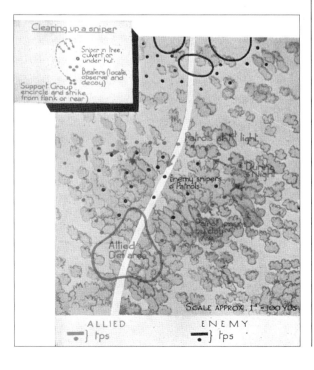

Weapons and equipment

In Malaya and Burma in 1941, there was a severe lack of weaponry and equipment. Any surplus quantities were channelled to the Home Forces training in Britain and those fighting in the Middle East and North Africa. For example, the 5/11th Sikh Regiment in Malaya was poorly equipped with mortars, Thompson sub-machine guns were received only in September 1941, and training in the weapons had yet to be undertaken.

Units had to adapt to the circumstances in which they found themselves. For instance in Malaya, instead of wearing standard khaki drill uniform the Argylls adopted long trousers, long-sleeved shirts, gym shoes and bush hats, all of which helped protect against leeches and malaria. Each patrol was given one Thompson sub-machine gun, a weapon that was considered extremely useful for close-quarter jungle fighting. The battalion was fairly well equipped for a

3in. mortar crews bombarding Meiktila. (IWM SE 3281)

unit in Malaya, with four Lanchester armoured cars, each equipped with two .303in. Vickers machine guns and a .5in. machine gun (the latter supposed to be effective against light armour), as well as three South African Marmon-Harringtons each with one Vickers and an anti-tank rifle. In addition the battalion had four 3in. and a few 2in. mortars. Each patrol was given a Thompson sub-machine gun as an alternative to the Sten, which, although useful for close-quarter fighting in the jungle, was prone to jamming and whose 9mm round was a little less effective than the Thompson.

Table 1: A comparison of tank numbers in the Far East theatre, October 1942 – March 1944			
Tank type	Numbers on 31 October 1942	Numbers on 31 March 1944 in India Command	Numbers on 31 March 1944 in South-East Asia Command
Light tanks	126		
Medium tanks			
Sherman		221	18
Cruiser tanks			
Stuart	146	719	106
Lee	79	325 [1]	267 [1]
Grant	169		
Infantry tanks			
Valentine	207		
Churchill	27		
Total	754	1,265	391

Notes

1 Figure includes both Lee and Grant types

In Burma, battalions were similarly ill-equipped. In 1940 the Burma Office had requested modern weapons for the British battalions but had been refused due to the shortage of Bren guns and mortars. All the India Office could spare was two Bren guns per battalion, although the minimum request for the two British battalions was four Brens, two anti-tank rifles, two 2in. mortars and 3in. mortars. As a result the forces in Burma were less prepared for war than those in Malaya. At the Battle of Sittang Bridge, World War I-vintage 18-pdr guns were still in use and Lewis Guns were used as anti-aircraft guns. Following the battle, when much of the weaponry and equipment was left behind, the army in Burma found itself poorly equipped, a state that continued for the remainder of the retreat. With regard to its artillery compliment, the army in Burma crossed the border into India with only ten 25-pdrs, eleven 3.7in. howitzers and four 2-pdr anti-tank guns.

After the retreat from Burma, various weapons were targeted as essential for jungle fighting, such as the *dhah*, an Indian knife used for clearing jungle undergrowth. It was realised that weapons had to be kept clean due to the problems of jamming in the moist jungle atmosphere, which hastened rusting and corrosion. The Cameron Report highlighted the value of the 2in. mortar and the range of the 3in. mortar, although the latter was less portable. Tanks were viewed as good for morale and effective for use in close support of the infantry. It was also realised that the uniform needed to be adapted; lightweight battledress and headdress, and rope-soled canvas boots were suggested.

Disease sorely undermined both morale and combat effectiveness. The casualty rate had reach over 10,000 a week by June 1943 and over half of these were due to malaria. The importance of anti-mosquito drill was acknowledged in AITM No. 21. All tents and shelters had to be sprayed before morning parade and all men were ordered to apply the anti-mosquito cream before leaving the tent. At evening parade all men were inspected by the officer in charge, to make sure the cream had been applied, and then the tents would be sprayed inside and out. Several pages of the AITM were devoted to jungle lore, helping soldiers to overcome any fear of the jungle by providing guidance on edible jungle foods, how much to drink, what clothes to wear, how to conduct movement and halts, how to maintain direction and orientation, health tips, and the hazards posed by cold nights, insects, and leeches. For instance, shorts were discouraged due to the danger of leeches. Light footwear, bush shirts, a floppy hat, a light haversack, rifle and minimal equipment were all advised, meaning that a soldier carried only about 20 lb and would not be overburdened in the jungle. It was also realised that weapons and equipment needed to withstand long periods of extreme humidity. For instance, composition containers for 2in. and 3in. mortar bombs would deteriorate, and any weapons and optical instruments containing wood would develop fungus growth after long periods in the jungle. Therefore, all equipment needed to be proofed against damp.

The first unit to convert to a jungle field regiment was 129th Field Regiment, but it found that neither the 3.7in. howitzer, with its range of 6,000 yds and 20 lb shell, nor the 3in. mortar were sufficiently powerful. The 25-pdr with a range of 13,400 yds and its versatility was considered essential, but it was too heavy to be towed by a jeep and too wide for jungle tracks and air mobility. The 129th Field Regiment experimented and found they could fit a jeep axle and wheels to the gun, which considerably improved movement in the jungle and air portability; this became known as the 'jury axle' 25-pdr.

The 25-pdr in action. The 25-pdr was developed during the 1930s and was in production by 1940. It was very adaptable and used in all theatres during World War II. It could fire high-explosive, smoke, and armour-piercing shells. (IWM SE 275)

When artillery support was not possible, 3in. and 2in. mortars provided essential firepower for the infantry. In fact, in the West African divisions whole mortar regiments were formed. Again the mortars were modified for use in the jungle; the base plate of the 3in. mortar was strengthened and a new sight installed to increase the range to 2,750 yds for the Mark 4 version. The Mark 5 was a specially designed lighter version for use in the Far East but only 5,000 had been produced by the end of the war. The 2in. was fixed with a 'bowed' plate in order to reduce its weight from 19 to 11 lbs without effecting its accuracy and range.

Later in the war, after the initial rejection of anti-tank weapons such as the .55in. Boys rifle by the British infantryman for fighting in the jungle, the PIAT was particularly effective against the entrenched Japanese bunkers. Other infantry weapons that proved equally effective included grenades, such as the No. 36 grenade or Mills bomb, and the plastic '77', which was a smoke grenade also used for clearing bunkers.

At the beginning of World War II, infantrymen were armed with the Short Magazine Lee Enfield .303in. Mark 3 pattern rifle. The Mark 4 had been issued to front-line troops in Europe by 1942, but few were in service in the Far East by 1944. India Command undertook further research into infantry rifles in order to make them smaller and lighter for easier handling in the jungle. The result was the precursor to the No. 5 Jungle Carbine, which was officially adopted by the War Office in September 1944, but was actually developed in India in 1943; however, the project was cancelled and very few were produced at the time. The No. 5 Mark 1 was 5in. shorter and 2 lb lighter. However, the No. 5 was not popular with the soldiers due to excessive recoil and its inaccuracy. It was declared obsolete in 1947.

A 3.7in. howitzer in action. It was originally developed for Indian mountain artillery and was particularly useful in the jungle as it could be quickly dismantled for transport by mule or by air. It was finally declared obsolete in 1960. (IWM SE 264)

The Lethbridge Mission, 1944

In June 1943, 202 Military Mission under Major-General J.S. Lethbridge, otherwise known as the Lethbridge Mission, began a tour of the south-west Pacific, New Guinea and Burma, as well as India, Australia, New Zealand and America, in order to research equipment and organisation needed to defeat the Japanese. The resulting report published in March 1944 recommended, among other things, the replacement of the 1937 pattern webbing, which was generally thought of as clumsy and uncomfortable in the jungle. The braces chafed collars and armpits and dragged on the shoulders, particularly if wet, and could also attract mould. The recommended webbing was meant to address these problems as it would be lighter, rot-proof, and with anti-corrosion metal fittings and an aluminium water bottle. The Mills Equipment Company designed new web equipment in early 1944, which was a single unit with larger pouches and crossed over at the back to prevent drag. Thus, there was now no need to tighten the belt, which increased comfort and ventilation. Inside the back of the haversack and the pack was a lining of oiled cotton to stop perspiration penetrating to the webbing. After modification this design was adopted for the 1944 pattern web equipment, but was not actually in service before the end of the war. The uniform adopted was a copy of the US Army field uniform with aertex being replaced by 'olive green' drill for the jacket and trousers. Similarly, other items were designed specifically for the Far East, such as mosquito nets for head and hands, lightweight blankets, jungle green puttees and canvas and rubber jungle boots, again based on the American issue. However, the Lethbridge recommendations were for the most part only put into practice for British troops earmarked to go to the Far East after victory had been achieved in Europe.

By 1944 the situation had considerably improved. Up to that point, troops had managed on the little they received and adapted its use to a jungle environment, such as dyeing equipment and uniforms jungle green. Weapons and equipment were in much better supply; for example, between September 1943 and April 1944, 2-pdr anti-tank gun numbers in theatre increased from 1,040 to 2,149, and wireless sets, which had been in very short supply in the early campaigns, increased from 8,781 to 21,849.

Bengal and Madras Sappers repair bomb damage on the Ngakyedauk Pass Road in the Arakan. British soldiers knew it as the 'Oke-Doke' Pass.

Command, control, communication, and intelligence

As a result of the lacklustre leadership shown during the First Arakan campaign, GHQ India made sweeping changes in senior staff officers and frontline commanders, in order to improve military effectiveness. The C-in-C India had initially appointed Major-General J. Bruce-Scott, former GOC 1st Burma Division, as Inspector of Infantry after the retreat from Burma. However, his experiences had exhausted him and rendered him ineffectual in his new role. After the Arakan, he was replaced by Major-General Reginald Savory, who had commanded 23rd Indian Division in Assam. Savory was responsible for training, organisation, arms and equipment, and made a critical contribution in all these areas.

General Slim examines a Japanese flag presented to him by the 7th Gurkha Rifles captured at Imphal. Note the 14th Army formation badge on his left shoulder, which was designed by Slim himself. (IWM IND 3620)

Major-General R.D. Inskip was appointed Inspector of Training Centres, in order to help the DMT, and he made a tour of all the centres to improve standards. For instance, the Regimental Centre of the 1st Punjab Regiment was visited in 1943 by most other training centres because of its high standards of jungle warfare training and its mock-up jungle; these ideas were later circulated. The overall result was the setting up of the Centres Organisation on 1 April 1943. The Centres now came under the control of GHQ India with an HQ that included specialist staff. They were renamed Regimental Centres and provided general training and holding battalions for the regiments; the CO of each centre was upgraded to a colonel. A new DMT was also appointed in May 1943, Major-General E.T.L. Gurdon. He was short of available training pamphlets and material and prior to taking up the post had asked for them to be sent to him as quickly as possible.

Most significantly, Wavell was appointed Viceroy of India and was replaced by General Claude Auchinleck as C-in-C India in June 1943. Operational control for campaigns was now to be conducted by the newly appointed Supreme Allied Commander in South-East Asia, Lord Louis Mountbatten. He was appointed in August but did not arrive in India until October 1943.

A change in front-line leadership was also made. The Arakan failure brought about the dismissal of Irwin, who was replaced by Lieutenant-General Sir George Gifford, a veteran of the bush fighting in East Africa during World War I. Later that year General 'Bill' Slim was appointed commander of 14th Army, and a range of experienced divisional commanders were also appointed.

The Indian High Command profited from the experiences of other Allied troops fighting jungle warfare: as noted previously, sections were included in the AITMs and the MTPs about US and Australian experiences. Also, in April 1943 Colonel Forster was made responsible for gathering information about

Admiral Lord Louis Mountbatten, Supreme Allied Commander SEAC, addressing British officers and men near the Arakan front. From 1943 onwards, troops were kept up to date on the current situation through conferences; this was so that they all felt part of a team fighting for the same objective and could see that their own individual roles in this were important. This included pep talks by senior commanders such as General Slim and Mountbatten, which were popular. One of Mountbatten's talks to the members of the 'forgotten' 14th Army was captured on film, and he commented that the 14th Army was not forgotten – rather no one had even heard of them! (IWM SE 6)

GHQ India

The above picture shows the formation badge of GHQ India; blue and red were the GHQ colours and the star is the emblem of India. GHQ was located in Delhi under the C-in-C India who commanded all British and Indian personnel of all three armed forces. The C-in-C was also the defence member on the Viceroy's Council and responsible for the Defence Department (renamed War Department in June 1942) as well as the three army commands of Northern, Eastern and Southern and Western Independent District. In April 1942, the then C-in-C, General Sir Archibald Wavell, reorganised this peacetime structure as it was no longer suitable. Thus, Central Command was set up under Lieutenant-General H.B.D. Willcox, which relieved the army commanders in the front line of internal security problems and took some of the responsibility for administration and training. The army commands remained Eastern and Southern and North-Western to include Northern command and Western District.

During the first two years of the war in the Far East, GHQ India was responsible for operations in Burma and the ensuing strategic problems. These duties were transferred to Admiral Lord Louis Mountbatten in November 1943 when he assumed command of the newly created South-East Asia Command. This left GHQ India responsible for the defence of the North-West Frontier, internal security, training and its role as a supply base.

In June 1943 General Sir Claude Auchinleck was appointed C-in-C India. He implemented the proposals of the recently convened Infantry Committee through the setting up of the training divisions and the concentration of GHQ India on jungle warfare. Auchinleck ensured that this was now the main focus for units, formations, reinforcements and training establishments throughout India. This new framework developed very quickly and by the end of 1943 India had developed a comprehensive training structure. The innovations instigated by Auchinleck and GHQ India were instrumental in the eventual defeat of the Japanese Army in the Burma campaign of 1944–45.

jungle warfare equipment for India Command on the British Army Staff at Washington and the resulting information was distributed to India Command, the War Office and Australia Command. In August 1943 the first of many jungle-warfare liaison letters passed between India Command and the Australian military forces, which later included the War Office in its circulation along with the New Zealand and US Commands. In addition, 50 Indian Army officers were sent to Australia. There they attended the Jungle Warfare School at Canungra and were then attached to fighting units in New Guinea. On their return to India some became instructors and others rejoined their units. In November a senior Australian officer, Brigadier Lloyd, who had fought in New Guinea and had been the commandant of the Australian Tactical School, was loaned to India Command for six months, during which time he visited and lectured to the 14th Army and schools such as the one at Shimoga.

The jungle made it difficult to retain control during a battle. Operations in Burma and Malaya had shown the importance of junior leaders, as command needed to be decentralised in the jungle; junior officers and NCOs had to make instant decisions without recourse to the chain of command. This was developed through training and practical experience, as often the responsibility for success or failure lay on the shoulders of these junior commanders.

Communications were difficult in the jungle as the wireless range was reduced and often failed at night. A different frequency at night was often required. Three types of radio were used in Burma: the No. 48, No. 19, and No. 22. The No. 48 set was a US version of the British No. 18 set; it was carried in a pack with a range of about 4 miles. The No. 19 set was used in armoured vehicles, and had a range

Men of the 4/6th Gurkha Rifles cross one of the many branches of the Irrawaddy with mule transports.

of 20 miles, or even further with the use of aerials. The No. 22 set was the standard all-arms radio of World War II. Liaison officers were also used, as were despatch riders who often worked in pairs.

The first Director of Military Intelligence in GHQ India, Major-General W.L. Cawthorne, was appointed in 1941. By the end of 1941 all formation HQs had a sizeable intelligence staff. In 1942 the Indian Intelligence Corps was set up. Other vital means of gathering intelligence included V Force and Z Force. V Force operated on the North-East Frontier in Naga, Kuki and Lushai villages grouped under civil or military offices or under paramilitary forces. An example of these includes the North Cactiar Watch and Ward, set up by the anthropologist Ursula Graham-Bower. All these were brought under military command and called V Force. Z Force comprised ex-Burma Army or forestry officers sent back into Burma to collect information.

An Indian Intelligence School was also set up in 1941 with three instructors, the Commandant, Major J. Campbell, Captain Majumda and Lieutenant A.A. Mains. The course run by the school concentrated on operational and air intelligence. Auchinleck appointed Colonel G.T. Wards as Commandant of the Intelligence School at Karachi in 1943. Wards, an expert on Japanese affairs who after the war went on to co-author the official history entitled *The War Against Japan*, had a realistic view of the strength of the Japanese Army. He gave a lecture in Singapore 1941, in which he warned of the network of Japanese spies in Malaya and of the efficiency of the Japanese Army – in stark contrast to the commonly held view at the time that it was vastly inferior to the British Army. General Bond, the then GOC Malaya, censored him after the talk: 'We must not discourage the chaps; we must keep their spirits up.'[11] The school ran a series of lectures on Burma and concentrated on the intelligence side of the war in the Far East. One lecture given was printed in *The Journal of the United Service Institution of India* in January 1943. This was one of the first instances of the periodical, the in-house journal of the army in India, publishing an article on jungle warfare. In the article Captain Edgar Peacock, who had been a forest officer in Burma, recommended that troops become accustomed to eating rice, travelling light, using camouflage and making a friend of the jungle. He

11 Papers of Colonel G.T. Wards, IWM 92/24/1.

A soldier of the 23rd Indian Division crosses the Lokhao River using a rope bridge.

suggested that one way of reducing the load carried was learning the different uses of bamboo such as for eating, drinking, making panjis and rafts and various other things. As a result of these lectures Peacock came to the attention of the DMT and was later sent to the Jungle Warfare School to lecture on jungle lore.

Men of the 2nd Survey Regiment, 25th Indian Division, climb up a 20ft-high tower used for locating enemy guns by flash-spotting.

Combat operations

The Battle of Kohima, March–May 1944

The growing ascendancy over the Japanese on the jungle battlefield was re-emphasised when the IJA made its main attack, Operation U-GO, in 1944. Its prime objective was the speedy capture of Imphal by 15th Army, under General Renya Mutaguchi, to forestall the imminent Allied invasion of Burma. The advance of the Japanese 33rd and 15th divisions began in early March. To the north, 31st Division was assigned the objective of Kohima in order to cut the Dimapur–Imphal road. This Japanese offensive had been expected, but not quite so soon, leaving the defending troops spreading out over a wide area: 17th Indian Division was in the Tiddim area, 50th Indian Parachute Regiment at Kohima, one brigade of 23rd Indian Division was near Ukrul, and 20th Indian Division was in the Kabaw Valley. They all had to withdraw in order to concentrate under IV Corps on the Imphal Plain to prevent Japanese infiltration. This withdrawal of large numbers of troops was in stark contrast to the early defeats of the British and Commonwealth armies in the Far East; here they carefully conducted tactical fighting withdrawals rather than pell-mell retreats. The 17th Indian Division, still commanded by Major-General 'Punch' Cowan, was not ordered to withdraw until 13 March though. As a result, they were cut off by the rapid Japanese advance. The 33rd Japanese Division marched against the 17th Indian Division and General Gracey's 20th Indian Division, and two brigades of 23rd Indian Division were called in to help the 17th retreat along the Tiddim Road. In addition, Slim decided that troops should be transferred from the Arakan front to ensure overwhelming superiority on the Imphal Plain. After their successes in the Arakan, both 5th and 7th Indian divisions travelled by air and train to the Imphal and Dimapur area.

The advancing 31st Japanese Division was held up by two battalions of the 50th Parachute Brigade at Ukrul and Sangshak, giving the garrison at Kohima essential time to build up their inadequate defences. The Kohima area was less densely covered by jungle than the previous battleground in the Arakan, being 5,000ft above sea level, surrounded by cultivated terraces, and with jungle-clad hills further away. The 161st Indian Infantry Brigade was sent into action immediately, with orders to protect Kohima and keep the vital supply route to Dimapur open. The 4th Battalion, Royal West Kent Regiment, together with a battery of the 24th Mountain Regiment and the 2nd Field Company, Indian Engineers, joined the garrison of mainly non-combatants or exhausted units retreating from the Chindwin River. The garrison was commanded by Colonel Hugh Richards and originally consisted of a battalion from the Assam Regiment, the paramilitary Assam Rifles, the Burma Regiment plus troops from the Reinforcement Camp, non-combatant troops who had not been

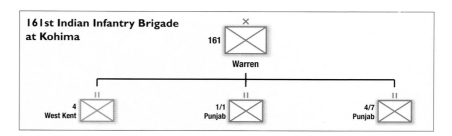

161st Indian Infantry Brigade at Kohima

161 — Warren

4 West Kent | 1/1 Punjab | 4/7 Punjab

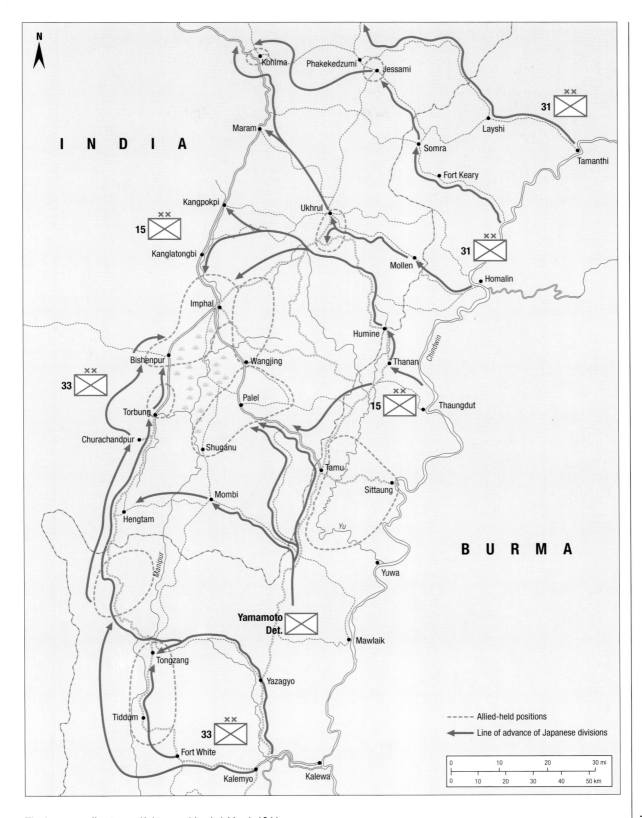

The Japanese offensive on Kohima and Imphal, March 1944.

The below photograph shows the key terrain features and positions that featured in the bloody and prolonged fighting at Kohima.

1. Deputy Commissioner's bungalow and tennis court
2. Garrison Hill
3. Kuki Piquet
4. Field Supply Depot (FSD) Hill
5. Detail Issue Store (DIS) Hill
6. Jail Hill
7. Road to Imphal
8. Pimple Hill
9. Congress Hill
10. General Purpose Transport (GPT) Ridge
11. Norfolk Ridge
12. Rifle Range
13. Two Tree Hill
14. Jetsoma Track
15. Pulebadze Peak (top right, 7,532ft.)
16. South end of Pulebadze Ridge
(Photo: IWM MH 3082A)

evacuated, and a battalion of untrained Nepalese State Forces. The Assam Regiment battalion was much depleted as they had also held up the Japanese advance on Kohima at Jessami. Defences were limited and there was little time for preparation, with few communication trenches and with water points outside the defence perimeter.

The remainder of 161st Indian Infantry Brigade were two miles away at Jotsoma, from where it provided decisive artillery support to the garrison, protected by the two infantry battalions, as the battery within the garrison was too restricted in space to use their guns and therefore acted as observation posts with wireless communication. One target was hit by 3,500 rounds in the space of five hours. As in the

Arakan, Japanese advances were again counter-attacked. Booby traps were laid when positions were given up, such as the approaches to Field Supply Depot (FSD) Hill. By 6 April the Japanese had taken most of Kohima, including Jail Hill from the depleted Assam Regiment.

Supplies were again air-dropped although the pilots had a much smaller drop zone. On 'Black 13th' the defenders saw their supplies dropped on the Japanese, the medical dressing unit received two direct hits, and the Rajputs on FSD Hill, who had managed to get to the Garrison before the road was cut, were forced from their positions by 75mm guns. Eventually, the defending troops were forced back from their positions until only Garrison Hill remained and they were fighting over the District Commissioner's tennis court.

The siege was over on the 18 April when the road was cleared by the 1/1st Punjab Regiment and the wounded and non-combatants were evacuated. The defenders had seen off 25 Japanese attacks in 14 days. The garrison was finally relieved by 6th Brigade of 2nd Division. General Giffard, C-in-C 11th Army Group, saw this early defence of Kohima as the turning point in the Japanese attack. A mixed group of trained and untrained troops successfully held off two Japanese regiments, the equivalent of two brigades, showing that their training and morale had improved considerably as compared to the earlier battles in Burma.

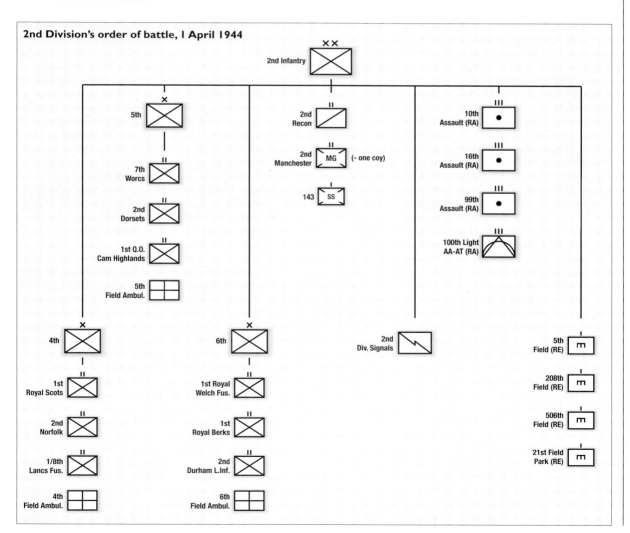

2nd Division's order of battle, 1 April 1944

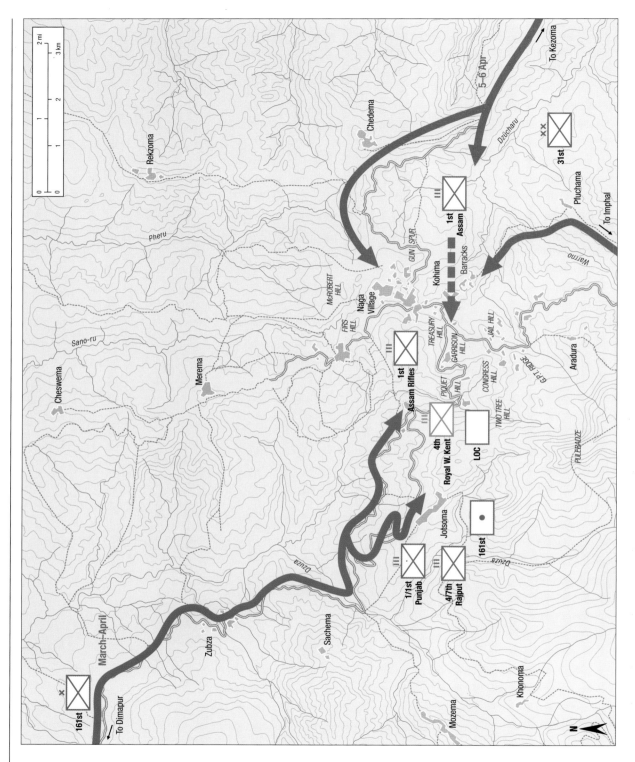

The opening moves of the Battle of Kohima, March–April 1944. Kohima occupied a vital position on the British supply road between Dimapur and Imphal. In mid-March the only British troops there were from the 1st Assam Rifles (initially stationed east of Kohima), Assam Regiment, and Line of Communication troops. Slim acted to reinforce Kohima, and moved the 161st Indian Brigade from Dimapur. The 4th Royal West Kent Regiment deployed around Garrison Hill, while the rest of the brigade and its artillery were initially placed in Jotsoma. The Japanese advance began on 5 April, but the tenacity of the defenders halted it, and a brief state of siege ensued for 13 days.

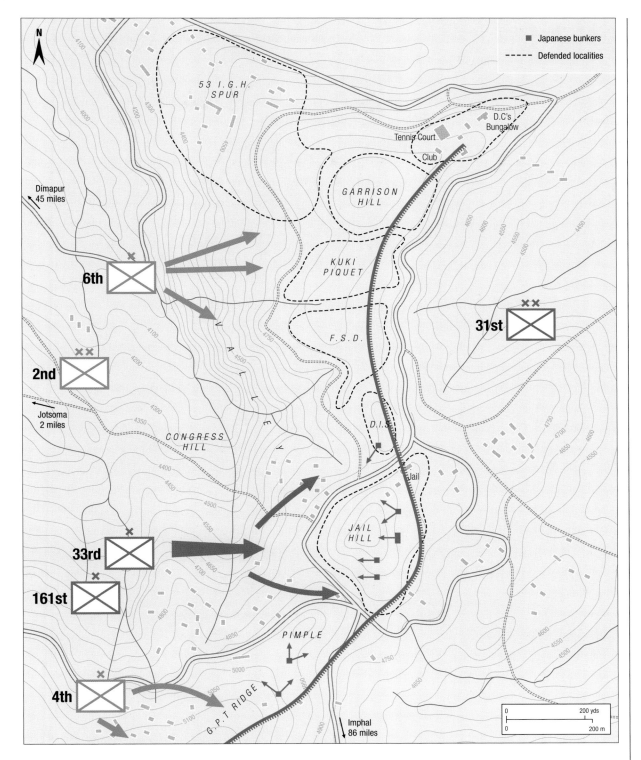

The British counter-attack at Kohima, May 1944. The British 2nd Division had been brought in as reinforcements, and its brigades were tasked with clearing Kohima of the Japanese. 4th Infantry Brigade was to destroy the enemy positions on G.P.T. Ridge to the south; 5th Infantry Brigade was to clear Naga Village via a north-east movement; and 6th Infantry Brigade was tasked with clearing the central Japanese positions. 33rd and 161st Indian Brigades were placed under 2nd Division's command to aid in the assault. By mid-May the Japanese had been forced to withdraw, and were in retreat.

The fighting at Kohima continued with the IJA now on the defensive and the 2nd Division trying to open the road. After this initial victory at Kohima, every hill and ridge had to be captured from the defending Japanese. One such action was the taking of Jail Hill. On 7 May the 1st Battalion of the Queen's Royal Regiment of 33rd Indian Infantry Brigade, now under the command of 2nd Division, were ordered to take Pimple Hill and Jail Hill, the latter being one of the largest features in central Kohima. Although no reconnaissance of the objective had been undertaken, it was realised that the plan depended on the well-defended GPT (General Purpose Transport) Ridge being cleared. These two features had previously eluded the efforts of the 2nd Division. The attack was to be in two parts. First to come was the capture of Pimple Hill by C Company after an artillery barrage, which was then lifted onto Jail Hill. D Company was then to pass through C Company and attack Jail Hill when the barrage had finished, followed by A Company, with B Company in reserve. The other two battalions of the brigade, 4/15th Punjab Regiment and 4/1st Gurkha Rifles, together with a battalion of the Royal Scots, would clear GPT Ridge.

Continual rain on the preceding night had made the going very tough for the advancing infantry, making visibility difficult and hampering forward movement. The Gurkhas and the Scots tried PIATs, 2in. smoke mortars, bazookas and grenades but came under attack from GPT Ridge. It was now clear that Jail Hill could not be taken unless GPT Ridge and DIS Hill were taken too. In addition tanks could not be brought in due to Japanese road blocks. A and D companies withdrew under artillery and mortar smoke and B company brought in the casualties. The battalion commander, Lieutenant-Colonel Duncombe, visited B Company the next day to inform them that the attack was not a failure as the battalion had captured its objectives even though the flanks were unprotected. He commented that he had ordered the withdrawal without recourse to higher command and the divisional commander, Major-General Grover, had called it a gallant effort.

A new plan was drawn up for another attack by the whole brigade as part of a divisional objective to clear the central hills of Kohima. GPT Ridge was to be taken by another brigade and then the Queen's Royal Regiment were to attack Jail Hill at first light whilst the 4/15th Punjabis were to capture DIS Hill, while the 1/1st Punjabis were to take Pimple the night before and then dig in. The Queen's plan was for C and B companies to attack the right and left of Jail Hill respectively with A and D companies following up. Jail and DIS Hills were to be bombarded by 25-pdrs and 3in. mortars, and support would come from divisional machine guns. Tanks were to fire on the west side of Jail Hill and help further if needed. Two bunker-destroying parties of the Indian Engineers were also available. For B Company's attack, 11 Platoon was on the right, with Major Lowry and tactical HQ in the centre; 10 Platoon on the right; and 12 Platoon behind. 11 Platoon was to take the bunkers on the top of the hill, 10 Platoon was to move to the left on the top and deal with any bunkers in the jail building area, with 12 Platoon in reserve.

For the attack the troops were given one day's ration and strict water discipline was maintained. Troops were to carry an extra five rounds of tracer

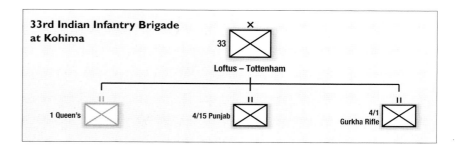

33rd Indian Infantry Brigade at Kohima

to indicate targets to the tanks. Packs were left at the start line and the rum issue was at the forming-up position. The regimental aid post was positioned between Pimple Hill and the main road, and casualties could be evacuated by stretcher or jeep to the advanced dressing station. Before B Company's attack they were shelled and suffered a number of casualties.

The attack took place on 11 May, with the battalion advancing under cover of darkness with heavy machine gun and artillery support. B Company got to the forming-up position at 3.15 a.m. The attack began at 5 a.m. When 10 Platoon got to the top of the hill, in under ten minutes, they caught a number of Japanese running down the hill to a bunker in the jail area but at the same time were fired upon from an enemy bunker further down the hill; 11 Platoon also came under attack from all directions. Although they managed to take one bunker, they also suffered a number of casualties. As a result Lowry ordered 12 Platoon to circle round to the right to attack the enemy's rear but they too encountered much enemy fire and got caught in a bunker. Then 11 and 12 platoons reorganised themselves into one platoon and held their ground, which overlooked the enemy. By midday, the company was organised as a platoon of 30 men, and dug in.

The battalion had overrun a few bunkers and held part of the hill, but the surrounding positions on GPT Ridge and DIS Hill remained in enemy hands. By the afternoon the north-west part of Jail Hill had been captured and the men of the Queen's Regiment had dug in, in mutually supporting positions. The battalion was reinforced by two companies of Gurkhas, who helped take more Japanese defensive posts and brought up some more grenades, supplies of which had been running low. During the night the rain poured down and by the next day there were just two bunkers left. One was shelled by tanks, which

An artist's impression of Jail Hill. (IWM IND 3929)

could not have been used earlier due to the poor weather and a Japanese roadblock. The tanks fired only 15 yds in front of the forward troops. The soldiers of the Queen's had to lie on their stomachs during the bombardment, but there were no casualties. The tanks then used their 75mm gun and automatic weapons, and a platoon occupied the bunker. The other bunker could not be reached by the tanks and was bombed with grenades by patrols; it was soon abandoned by the Japanese defenders. After the capture of the hill it was found that the main bunker had steel shutters to counter grenades and could hold 50 Japanese troops; there were also 20 other bunkers on Jail Hill. On 14 May the Queen's were relieved by a Punjabi battalion.

A memorial to all ranks of the 1st Battalion, the Queen's Royal Regiment who died in the battles for Jail Hill was made by the Battalion Pioneers and unveiled on 31 August 1944 by Lieutenant-General Stopford, GOC XXXIII Indian Corps. The memorial fell into disrepair and was finally replaced in 1972 by another in the Commonwealth War Graves Commission cemetery at Kohima.

The centre of Kohima had now been cleared. On 22 May 33rd Brigade took over the Naga village area. The Queen's were in the south-east of the perimeter, with the 4/15th Punjabis on their left, and the 4/1st Gurkhas on the right. The Japanese positions were only about 100 yds away and the situation was said to resemble the trench warfare of World War I. On 26 May the enemy attacked in strength but was repulsed by the brigade, and fighting continued until 31 May, when B Company eventually took Church Knoll. On 1 June the battalion was withdrawn to Dimapur for rest and reinforcement. The battalion suffered heavily at Kohima with 4 officers and 65 other ranks killed, and 6 officers and 118 other ranks wounded. The Japanese had conducted a fanatical defence around Kohima; it took 2nd Division and 33rd Indian Infantry Brigade until June to clear the area of Japanese troops, who held on in their bunkers and defensive positions.

The fighting around Imphal

Fighting around Imphal continued during this period at considerable intensity. The 33rd Japanese Division was still fighting 17th Indian Division to the south-west of Imphal at Bishenpur, together with a brigade of 20th Indian Division; the rest of the 20th was at Shenan. 5th Indian Division at Ukhrul, with the 23rd Indian Division in reserve, was up against the Japanese 15th Division.

The Japanese came closest to success on 6 April when they captured the commanding heights around Nunshigum, which overlooked Imphal. This was the nearest the IJA would get to Imphal. It was taken from a detachment of the 3/9th Jats, but the remainder of the battalion retook it later that day. On 11 April the Japanese retook the position. The Allied counter-attack came two days later, when the hill was bombarded by dive-bombers, fighter-bombers and artillery. The hill was retaken in a famous action by the 3rd Carabiniers and a battalion of the 1/17th Dogras, when all the officers became casualties and the attack was led by NCOs. The action at Nunshigum showed that the use of initiative and the importance of junior leadership learnt during training proved very effective.

In the counter-offensive against the Japanese forces, 5th Indian Division advanced up the Imphal–Kohima road. 20th Indian Division held the hills of Crete West and Scraggy and were relieved by the 23rd, who pushed the Japanese out of the Shenan Area. 17th Indian Division got the better of the Japanese 33rd Division, against whom they had fought in the 1942 retreat.

On 22 June the Dimapur Road was reopened when 2nd Division met up with troops of 5th Indian Division, 29 miles north of Imphal. The battles for Kohima and Imphal were over and the Commonwealth forces had inflicted a crushing defeat on the IJA. They had inflicted 53,505 casualties on the Japanese 15th Army, whose overall strength had been 84,280, in contrast to 16,700 casualties among the Commonwealth forces. In addition, the 14th

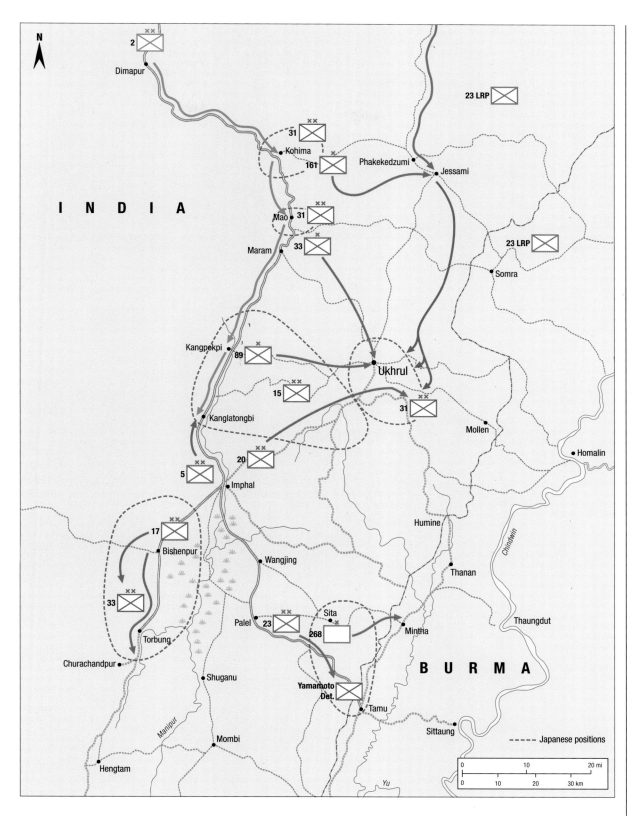

The British counter-offensive, June–July 1944.

A view of the Imphal Plain from the Ukhrul Road.

Army had captured 11 guns and 20 tanks. General Slim commented in a letter to a friend, Lieutenant-Colonel H.R.K. Gibbs; 'there is no doubt about it that the old Fourteenth Army has given him [IJA] the biggest defeat he has ever had in his whole history'.[12]

12 Letter from General W. Slim to Lt.-Col. H. R. K. Gibbs, 15 August 1944, IWM, Misc 54 item 824.

Lessons learned

The disastrous Malayan campaign of 1941–42 was a shocking defeat for British arms. It was carefully analysed by British officers and it quickly became apparent that 'milking' was a fundamental problem affecting all British and Indian units. They were also eager to discern lessons for troops in Burma and those under training. Early lessons were incorporated into a revised edition of MTP No. 9 in January 1942. This training manual discussed the Japanese infiltration and outflanking tactics and the use of local disguise by the Japanese forces, which made it very difficult for Commonwealth troops to recognise them. The Japanese troops travelled lightly and made good use of tanks, which had previously been discounted by Malaya Command as they had been seen as unsuitable for the terrain. It remarked on the use of Japanese snipers who used chained dogs to give warning of any approaching enemy. It maintained that the main defence against these Japanese tactics and ruses in the jungle was defence in depth, more mobile and less heavily laden troops, good fire discipline, withdrawal and immediate counter-attacking.

The early lessons from Malaya were also incorporated into the Army in India Training Memorandum (AITM) series that was used in India to disseminate the latest tactical lessons and training information. AITM No. 14 published in February 1942 reiterated the general lessons from Malaya, such as keeping equipment to a minimum, a single light machine gun per platoon, the issuing of rifles or Thompson sub-machine guns to all soldiers, good fire discipline, frontal attacks only as fixing operations, and immediate counter-attacks. The example of the Argylls' action at Grik Road was cited, where the Japanese became a 'herd' once they lost the initiative, showing that the Argylls' training methods were successful. It demonstrated that static defence was inappropriate in the jungle and that defence in depth was essential to prevent any encircling movements. At Grik, for example, the Argylls operated at a depth of eight or nine miles. Accordingly, the ratio of casualties was five to one in the Argylls' favour. The April 1942 AITM listed the three most important lessons from Malaya as being the passing on of information, patrolling, and high standards of physical fitness and discipline. Areas where specialised training were seen as lacking were road discipline, anti-aircraft small arms defence, anti-tank defence, concealment and the lack of offensive spirit. There was little mention of jungle training, but rather a general need for the toughening up of troops.

The British High Command made an immediate effort to learn from the debacle in Malaya, ensuring that trained and experienced officers and specialists were evacuated. Brigadier Stewart and three other Argylls – Major Angus Rose, Captain David Wilson and CSM Arthur Bing – were evacuated from Singapore to impart their knowledge to units in India. En route Stewart also passed on his knowledge to the Australians in Java and on the voyage to Ceylon. Indeed, it is

Dakotas dropping supplies to the 5th Indian Division on the Tiddim Road. Air supply was vital to the success of the campaign in Burma. One of the first successful air supply drops on the North-East Frontier was carried out to Soutcol at Kyauktaw. Previously air supply had been used on the North-West Frontier and in the First Chindit operation. (IWM IND 3966)

generally accepted by Australian and British historians that it was Stewart's experience, rather than Gordon Bennett, which helped to advance the learning curve in jungle warfare in the Australian Army. It was following consultation with Stewart that the Australians produced a pamphlet on Japanese tactics in Malaya, which was distributed throughout the Australian Army.

The Argylls made lecture tours of India. Stewart also made a radio broadcast about the campaign to build up morale, and prepared a report. Major Richard Storry, another evacuee from Singapore, attended a lecture by Stewart at the Intelligence School at Karachi and commented:

> The lecture was a most outspoken, in parts bitter indictment of the higher planning and conduct of operations in Malaya. Mistakes of strategy and tactics were analysed, Jap methods described and Col Stewart's own theories of counteracting them explained. It was a merciless post-mortem which impressed us all. This lecture Stewart gave, I heard, up and down India that spring 1942. Later he was one of those who directed the training of units for operations in Burma; so much, I think, is owed to him.[13]

Following the completion of the lecture tours in India, the evacuated Argylls made up No. 6 GHQ Training Team, which organised training exercises and lectures for 14th Indian Division and 2nd Division. Apart from Stewart the other Argylls remained in India to instruct. Rose was in the training team until 1943 and then set up the Jungle Warfare Training Centre at Raiwala, before commanding a battalion of the King's Own Scottish Borderers in Burma. Captain David Wilson and CSM Bing became chief instructors at 2nd Division's Battle School at Poona. On Stewart's return to the UK, his report on the lessons from Malaya was reprinted for use by the UK Home Forces. Stewart was back in the Far East by 1944, when he was appointed Brigadier General Staff 11th Army Group with responsibility for training.

Several other officers who had fought in the campaign also wrote detailed reports pinpointing the lessons learned. Brigadier Carpendale, CO 28th Indian Infantry Brigade, was another officer evacuated from Singapore, and his findings also noted the importance of jungle training. Some war correspondents also studied the lessons from Malaya. Ian Morrison, correspondent for *The Times*, was the first to publish some very clear lessons from the disaster. As early as May 1942 he noted in his *Malayan Postscript* that the Japanese had learnt the art of encirclement after years of fighting the Chinese who had developed these enveloping tactics against invaders. Morrison also highlighted the way they deceived defending forces by wearing Malay and Chinese costume; their survival on minimal food, mainly a diet of rice; and their use of natural resources such as rivers, aided by local guides and transport such as bicycles. He stressed their use of weapons particularly suited to the jungle, such as the 2in. mortar and hand grenades. He also stressed the importance of training for jungle warfare to counteract the efficiency of the Japanese in the jungle.

The majority of the reports on Malaya were drawn up for Major H.P. Thomas, who prepared a detailed and influential report for the C-in-C during the early summer of 1942. In this process he also interviewed over a hundred officers. The findings did state that a detailed account would never be available due the destruction of official records prior to capitulation. All the reports from Malaya hammered home the importance of appropriate minor tactics and training for jungle fighting. It was now up to the high command to put this into practice.

The lessons of the retreat from Burma were closely studied in India as soon as Burcorps had escaped, as arguably it provided far more relevant information

---

13 Major G.R. Storry, *Service with the Intelligence Corps in India and Burma March 1942–May 1943* (Unpublished Memoir, 1946–1947), Storry Mss., IWM 01/34/2, 6/10.

than the events in Malaya. It was generally acknowledged that failure in Burma was due in large part to a lack of training in jungle warfare. 7th Armoured Brigade was an exception in that it had not undergone any jungle training; however, its role was mainly limited to the roads and it was only involved in the operations after the fall of Rangoon, in the open plains of Burma rather than in the earlier jungle battles. Other formations such as the 48th Indian Infantry Brigade under Brigadier Cameron performed admirably after experience in the jungle, particularly when his brigade adopted the tactic of 'all round defence' in the jungle. The lack of military intelligence, the low priority of the Burma front, the 'milking' of British, Indian and Burmese battalions, the swapping of command between Burma, the War Office, GHQ India and ABDA Command, and the decision to decline an offer of more Chinese divisions, all contributed to the defeat in Burma. The lack of jungle-

Major Wako Lisanori of 28th Army hands his sword to Lieutenant-Colonel Smyth of 1/10th Gurkha Rifles, 63rd Brigade, 17th Indian Division, at Abya in August 1945.

trained troops, however, was the most decisive factor in the defeat in the view of many of the participants. In fact, the previous training of the Indian Army had been inadequate for the jungle conditions of Burma, because the little training that 17th Indian Division had undergone was geared towards desert warfare.

Tactical lessons learnt in Burma differed from those in Malaya. For instance, flanking movements were seen as difficult to support and beyond the abilities of the war-trained army whereas the importance of overwhelming firepower was realised in defeating roadblocks. In attack 'Blitz' tactics were successful, where light machine gunners and those with Thompson sub-machine guns led the attack with riflemen following. The importance of patrolling was acknowledged but better communications, maps and intelligence were needed to make patrols more successful in the jungle. Finally, rather than detailed orders, conferences and the issue of instructions were seen as ways to decentralise command on very mobile fronts; junior leadership was seen as the key to success against the Japanese in the jungle.

The most detailed investigation was produced soon after the arrival in the Imphal Plain; Major-General Cowan, GOC 17th Indian Division, instructed Brigadier Cameron and a committee of battalion commanders to identify new training, tactics and equipment needed to fight successfully in Burma. The committee produced the Cameron Report, which recognised that training in the jungle was vital; movement and control in the jungle became second nature, and all arms had to be trained in jungle warfare and be responsible for their own protection. All the lessons from Malaya and Burma were eventually encapsulated into the third edition of the jungle warfare training pamphlet MTP No. 9.

The First Arakan campaign was yet another dismal failure with defeat inflicted on Commonwealth troops by a numerically inferior force. However, lessons were learnt at actions such as Donbaik, and these gave troops valuable first-hand experience of jungle warfare (with its poor visibility, and patterns of quiet days with some shelling and mortaring followed by main Japanese attacks coming in at night). General Wavell and Lieutenant General Irwin attributed the failure to poor regimental command and the lack of training, which in fact reflected badly on themselves rather than on their subordinates. This situation was not helped by Wavell's continued underestimation of the Japanese Army, a common fault prior to the Japanese invasion of South-East Asia; he could not understand why the Indian Army could not defeat it.

Administrative problems were vast considering the large distances involved. Pack transport was the main source of supplies and this depended on reasonable weather to keep the routes passable. One of the first successful air supply drops on the North-East Frontier was carried out during the First Arakan. The adoption of air supply, when sufficient transport planes became available, formed a solution to the supply difficulties. Generally supplies got through, but it was a very slow process. A number of lessons were learnt in this area, such as the importance of basic jungle-warfare training, the arming of all the administrative units, the need for a special ration to be used in emergencies for periods of up to a week, the need to encourage living off the land, and the use of air supply to counteract enveloping tactics.

The Arakan campaign had been a tactical failure. Repeated attacks on a narrow front against the bunkers had proved disastrous at an early stage, and the encircling tactics employed by the Japanese at the end of the campaign had again proved decisive. It was now realised that artillery, tank or air support was needed for attacks against these entrenched positions. Infantry weapons needed adjustment; for instance, anti-tank rifles could be kept in reserve and fewer 3in. mortars should be carried (due to the weight of the ammunition). Patrolling was seen as being of paramount importance in attack and defence, and defences had to be secure. The outstanding failure of the campaign noted by most reports was the overall low level of training and the very low standard of training of reinforcements. Large numbers were needed but were arriving from regimental depots with little basic training, let alone jungle warfare training. Generally, the First Arakan caused military and civilian morale in India to plummet. The myth of the Japanese superman in the jungle was at its peak and questions were raised as to whether the Indian Army would ever be capable of defeating the Japanese.

The Infantry Committee led the way in the development of jungle warfare doctrine and training by proposing the setting up of the training divisions and the need for a centralised doctrine for jungle warfare. These proposals were put into practice by General Auchinleck and GHQ India. All training establishments in India were now re-orientated to teach jungle warfare and produced a supply of jungle-trained instructors, cadres and complete units. This new training structure developed very quickly and by the end of 1943 India had a comprehensive structure in place. This undoubtedly played a key role in the defeat of the Japanese Army.

The fighting in the Arakan, Imphal and Kohima areas bore out the importance of jungle training as well as air superiority, organised logistics and good leadership. It showed what resolute jungle-trained troops, with confidence in themselves and their leaders, could achieve in battle. The actions at the Admin Box, Jail Hill, Nunshigum, Kohima and Imphal demonstrated the successful use of infiltration tactics and aggressive patrolling when fighting in dense jungle against the IJA. It showed the benefits of tank, artillery and air co-operation and demonstrated the resolve of support units, all of which was made possible with thorough jungle training. Even though the jungle was a difficult environment, it was no longer one that caused alarm or fear among Commonwealth soldiers. The troops of the 14th Army had grown considerably in confidence and were no longer afraid of this environment or the Japanese, and they displayed increasing battlefield effectiveness with aggressive tactics in both defence and attack.

The 14th Army was by no means perfect by the summer of 1944, but now had the upper hand over the Japanese. The divisions were prepared for the next phase of the fighting and absorbed the lessons of the recent operations. They were not only trained for jungle warfare but also for air-mobile and amphibious operations, and for the open warfare on the central plains of Burma.

Training and doctrine were not the only factors in the re-conquest of Burma and inflicting the biggest land defeat on the Japanese Army. Equipment was no longer in short supply in SEAC by the summer of 1944, in contrast to the previous low priority accorded to this theatre. The troops had managed on the little they received, and adapted its use to the jungle environment, such as dyeing equipment and uniforms jungle green. Also, as Louis Allen has pointed out, the battles in Burma were not won solely in the jungle; the later victories were fought in the open. Other factors that were crucial in the defeat of the Japanese included improved logistics and air supply, medical advances and health discipline, artillery, tank and air support, high morale and good leadership.

The recognition of the need for training in jungle fighting, a jungle-warfare doctrine and extensive jungle experience in World War II aided the British Army in later campaigns in the Far East. During the Malayan Emergency 1948–60, Ferret Force, a scratch unit of British, Gurkha and Malay troops who had fought in the jungle during World War II, discovered 12 Communist guerrilla camps in 1948. It was also reflected in the careers of General Sir Walter Walker and Colonel John Cross. Walker was an operational director in the Malayan campaign and the director of operations during the Borneo Confrontation 1962–66. He set up the Jungle Warfare School in Johore, which was run by Cross for a long period, both having served their jungle apprenticeships in Burma.

Chronology

1941

19 February	8th Australian Division lands in Singapore.
2 December	Force Z, consisting of HMS *Prince of Wales*, HMS *Repulse* and four destroyers, arrives in Singapore.
8 December	Japanese forces invade Malaya and attack Pearl Harbor, Hawaii. Britain and the United States declare war on Japan.
10 December	HMS *Prince of Wales* and HMS *Repulse* are sunk off the eastern coast of Malaya.
11 December	The Battle of Jitra takes place.
18–19 December	Japanese troops invade Hong Kong.
19 December	The Battle of Grik Road.
25 December	Hong Kong surrenders.

1942

7 January	The Battle of Slim River.
11 January	The Japanese Army captures Kuala Lumpur.
15 January	General Wavell assumes command of ABDA (American British Dutch Australian) Command.
20 January	The Japanese 15th Army invades Burma.
23 January	Japanese troops land in New Guinea and the Solomon Islands.
29 January	The British 18th Division arrives in Singapore.
30 January	British and Commonwealth forces withdraw to Singapore.
31 January	The Japanese capture Moulmein, Burma.
7 February	General Percival, GOC Malaya Command, declares that Singapore will be held to the last man.
8 February	Japanese forces cross the Johore Straits.
15 February	Singapore surrenders.
21 February	British and Commonwealth troops withdraw to Sittang Bridge.
22–23 February	The Battle of the Sittang River.
27 February	The Battle of Java Sea.
5 March	General Alexander is appointed GOC Burma.
8 March	The retreat from Rangoon begins.
10 March	General Stilwell is appointed Chief of Staff to Generalissimo Chiang Kai-shek in China.
16 March	General Slim is appointed corps commander of Burcorps.
17 March	General MacArthur is appointed Supreme Commander, Allied Forces, South-East Pacific.
19 March	General Slim is appointed corps commander in Burma.
1 May	The British evacuate Mandalay.
15 May	British and Commonwealth forces retreat across the India–Burma border.
4–7 June	The Battle of Midway.
7–8 August	American forces land on Guadalcanal.
5 September	Australian forces defeat the Japanese at Milne Bay in New Guinea.
21 September	The First Arakan campaign begins.

1943

14 February	The First Chindit operation begins.
17 March	The Japanese counter-attack in the Arakan.
18 April	The Chindits cross the Irrawaddy River.

12 May	The disastrous First Arakan campaign ends.
18 June	General Wavell is appointed Viceroy of India, and is replaced as C-in-C India by General Auchinleck.
25 August	Admiral Lord Louis Mountbatten is appointed Supreme Allied Commander in South-East Asia.
7 October	Mountbatten arrives in India.
21 October	Subhas Chandra Bose forms the 'Government of Free India' in Singapore.

1944

9 January	The Second Arakan campaign begins.
5 February	The Second Chindit operation begins.
6–27 February	The Battle of Admin Box.
15 March	The Japanese U-GO offensive on the Imphal Plain begins.
24 March	General Orde Wingate is killed in a plane crash.
29 March	The siege of Imphal begins.
4 April	The Japanese attack on Kohima begins.
20 April	The siege of Kohima is broken.
3 June	The Battle of Kohima ends.
22 June	The Kohima–Imphal road is cleared.
3 August	The Japanese withdraw from Myitkyina.
27 August	The last Chindits are evacuated to India.
28 September	The Third Arakan campaign begins.
28 October	Stilwell is replaced by General Wedemeyer in China and by General Sultan in Burma.
2 December	14th Army takes Kalewa.

1945

10 January	14th Army takes Shwebo.
22 January	The Burma Road to China is re-opened.
12 February	14th Army begins main operations across the Irrawaddy River.
19 February	US Marines land on Iwo Jima.
4 March	The Battle of Meiktila takes place.
9 March	14th Army enters Mandalay.
13 March	Maymo is recaptured.
15 March	The Japanese counter-attack at Meiktila.
20 March	14th Army recaptures Mandalay.
1 April	US 10th Army lands on Okinawa.
28 April	The Arakan is retaken.
3 May	Rangoon is retaken.
10 May	14th Army links up with XV Corps in the Arakan, cutting off Japanese troops west of the Irrawaddy.
28 May	14th Army withdraws to India and British 12th Army establishes HQ at Rangoon.
1 June	Mountbatten announces his intent to attack Singapore on 9 September (Operation Zipper).
15 June	A victory parade is held in Rangoon.
4 July	General MacArthur announces the liberation of the Philippines.
6 August	The first atomic bomb ('Little Boy') is dropped on Hiroshima.
8 August	The Soviet Union declares war on Japan.
9 August	The second atomic bomb ('Fat Man') is dropped on Nagasaki.
14 August	Japan agrees to an unconditional surrender.
2 September	General MacArthur accepts the surrender of the Japanese at Tokyo Bay on board USS Missouri flanked by generals Percival and Wainwright, who had been prisoners of war of the Japanese.
12 September	Mountbatten accepts the surrender of the Japanese forces in South-East Asia at Singapore.
13 September	The Japanese sign the surrender for Burma.

Bibliography

Allen, Louis *Burma: The Longest War 1941–1945* (London, Dent, 1984)

Allen, Louis *Singapore, 1941–1942* (London, Davis-Poynter, 1972)

Anglim, Simon 'Orde Wingate and the Theory behind the Chindit Operations: Some Recent Findings', *Journal of the Royal United Services Institute*, Vol. 147, No. 2 (April 2002)

Bond, Brian and Tachikawa, Kyoichi (ed.) *British and Japanese Military Leadership in the Far Eastern War 1941–1945* (London, Frank Cass, 2004)

Callahan, Raymond *Burma 1942–1945* (London, Davis-Poynter, 1978)

Callahan, Raymond 'The Jungle, the Japanese and the Sepoy' (Unpublished paper, 1997)

Chong, Ong Chit *Operation Matador: Britain's War Plans against the Japanese 1918–1941* (Singapore, Times Academic Press, 1997)

Colvin, John *No Ordinary Men: The Story of the Battle of Kohima* (London, Leo Cooper, 1995)

Doulton, A.J. *The Fighting Cock: Being the History of the 23rd Indian Division 1942–1947* (Aldershot, Gale & Polden, 1951)

Elliott, Major General J.G. *A Roll of Honour* (London, Cassell, 1965)

Evans, Geoffrey and Brett-James, Anthony *Imphal: A Flower on Lofty Heights* (London, Macmillan, 1962)

Farndale, General Sir Martin *History of the Royal Regiment of Artillery: The Far East Theatre 1941–1946* (London, Brasseys, 2002)

Ferris, John '"Worthy of Some Better Enemy?": The British Estimate of the Imperial Japanese Army, 1919–1941, and the Fall of Singapore' *Canadian Journal of History*, Vol. XXVII (August 1993)

Fraser, George Macdonald *Quartered Safe Out Here* (London, Harvill, 1992)

French, David *Raising Churchill's Army: The British Army and the War against Germany 1919–1945* (Oxford, Oxford University Press, 2000)

GHQ India, MTP No. 9 (India), *The Jungle Book* (4th edition, September 1943)

Jeffreys, Alan '"The Jungle Book": Jungle Training in South East Asia, 1941–1943', *Imperial War Museum Review*, No. 12 (1999)

Jeffreys, Alan *Jungle Warfare Doctrine and Training of the British and Indian Infantry in South East Asia, 1941–1944*, University of London, M.Phil. thesis (2003)

Kempton, Chris *'Loyalty & Honour': The Indian Army September 1939 – August 1947* (Milton Keynes, Military Press, 2003)

Kirby, Major-General S. Woodburn *History of the Second World War: The War Against Japan* (London, HMSO, 1957–1969), Vols. 1–5.

Kirby, Major-General S. Woodburn *Singapore: The Chain of Disaster* (London, Cassell, 1971)

Lewin, Ronald *Slim the Standard Bearer* (London, Leo Cooper, 1976)

Lodge, A.B. *The Fall of Gordon Bennett* (Sydney, Allen & Unwin, 1986)

Lowry, Michael *An Infantry Company in Arakan and Kohima* (Aldershot, Gale & Polden, 1950)

Lowry, Michael *Fighting through to Kohima: A Memoir of War in India and Burma* (Barnsley, Leo Cooper, 2003)

Lunt, James *The Retreat from Burma* (Newton Abbot, David & Charles, 1989)

Mackenzie, Compton *Eastern Epic* (London, Chatto & Windus, 1951)

Marston, Daniel *Phoenix from the Ashes: The Indian Army in the Burma Campaign* (Westport, Connecticut, Praeger, 2003)

Mason, Philip *A Matter of Honour: An Account of the Indian Army and its Men* (London, Cape, 1974)

Masters, John *The Road Past Mandalay* (London, Michael Joseph, 1961)

Matthews, Geoffrey *The Re-Conquest of Burma 1943–1945* (Aldershot, Gale & Polden, 1966)

Maule, Henry *Spearhead General: The Epic Story of General Sir Frank Messervy and his men in Eritrea, North Africa and Burma* (London, Odhams, 1961)

Moffat, Jonathan and Holmes McCormack, Audrey *Moon over Malaya: A Tale of Argylls and Marines* (Glasgow, Coombe Publishing, 1999)

Moreman, T.R. *The Jungle, the Japanese and the British Commonwealth Armies at War in South East Asia, 1941–1945* (London, Taylor & Francis, 2004)

Moreman, T.R. 'The Jungle, the Japanese and the Australian Army: Learning the Lessons of New Guinea, 1942–1944' (unpublished paper, 2001)

Moreman, T.R. '"Small Wars" and "Imperial Policing": The British Army and the Theory and Practice of Colonial Warfare in the British Empire, 1919–1939', *Journal of Strategic Studies*, Vol. 19, No. 4 (December, 1996)

Morrison, Ian *Malayan Postscript* (London, Faber & Faber, 1942)

Murfett, Malcolm et al. *Between Two Oceans: A Military History of Singapore from First Settlement to Final British Withdrawal* (Oxford, Oxford University Press, 1999)

Neild, Eric *With Pegasus in India: The Story of the 153 Gurkha Parachute Battalion* (Singapore, nd)

Perrett, Bryan *Tank Tracks to Rangoon: The Story of British Armour in Burma* (London, Robert Hale, 1992)

Perry, F.W. *The Commonwealth Armies: Manpower and Organisation in Two World Wars* (Manchester, Manchester University Press, 1988)

Roberts, Michael *Golden Arrow: The Story of the 7th Indian Division in the Second World War* (Aldershot, Gale & Polden, 1952)

Robertson, G.W. *The Rose and Arrow: A Life Story of 136th (1st West Lancashire) Field Regiment, Royal Artillery 1939–1946* (136th Field Regiment Old Comrades Association, 1986)

Slim, Field Marshal the Viscount William *Defeat into Victory* (London, Cassell, 1956)

Smurthwaite, David (ed.) *The Forgotten War: The British Army in the Far East 1941-1945* (London, National Army Museum, 1992)

Stewart, Brigadier I.M. *The Thin Red Line: 2nd Argylls in Malaya* (London, Nelson, 1947)

Swinson, Arthur *Kohima* (London, Cassell, 1966)

Tsuji, Colonel Masanobu *Japan's Greatest Victory, Britain's Worst Defeat* (Staplehurst, Spellmount, 1997)

Warren, Alan *Singapore 1942: Britain's Greatest Defeat* (London, Hambledon, 2002)

Wilson, David *The Sum of Things* (Staplehurst, Spellmount, 2001)

Wiseman, Lieutenant-Colonel D.J.C. *The Second World War 1939–1945 Army: Special Weapons and Types of Warfare* (London, HMSO, 1952)

List of abbreviations

A & MT	Animal & Mechanical Transport
AA-AT	Anti-Aircraft and Anti-Tank
ABDA	American British Dutch Australian
AITM	Army in India Training Memorandum
BFF	Burma Frontier Force
BMP	Burma Military Police
Bn	Battalion
Bty	Battery
C-in-C	Commander-in-Chief
CO	Commanding Officer
Coy	Company
CSM	Company Sergeant Major
DMT	Director of Military Training
ECO	Emergency Commissioned Officer
GHQ	General Headquarters
GOC	General Officer Commanding
GSO1	General Staff Officer Grade 1
GSO2	General Staff Officer Grade 2
HK&S	Hong Kong and Singapore
IE	Indian Engineers
ISF	Indian State Forces
IJA	Imperial Japanese Army
L of C	Lines of Communication
MTP	Military Training Pamphlet
NCO	Non-Commissioned Officer
RA	Royal Artillery
RAF	Royal Air Force
RASC	Royal Army Service Corps
RE	Royal Engineers
Regt	Regiment
RIASC	Royal Indian Army Service Corps
S & M	Sappers & Miners
SEAC	South East Asia Command
TU	Training Unit
WA	West African

Index